Modern Gikuyu Dictionary
Gikuyu-English
English-Gikuyu

kasahorow

Read Gikuyu. Every day
1st Printing

www.kasahorow.org

Auntie Dorcas

Contents

How to use this dictionary

Hello! This dictionary is created to help you learn better! Keep it by your side when reading English and Gikuyu books.

If you are reading and you never have to use a dictionary, then it means you are ready to read more advanced texts! Well done!

Entries in this dictionary are arranged alphabetically in both the GIKUYU-ENGLISH section and the ENGLISH-GIKUYU section. Here is the Gikuyu alphabet to jog your memory:

Aa	Bb	Cc	Dd	Ee	Gg
Hh	Ii	Ĩĩ	Jj	Kk	Mm
Nn	Oo	Rr	Tt	Uu	Ũũ
Ww	Yy				

Here are some abbreviations used in this dictionary to show you the function of the word in a sentence:

Abbreviation	Meaning
n	A **noun** is a name
adj	An **adjective** shows the quality of a noun
p	A **pronoun** points to a noun
v	A **verb** is an action
adv	An **adverb** shows the intensity of a verb

We wish you many happy reading adventures in English and Gikuyu!

kasahorow

Modern Gikuyu

Modern Gikuyu is a more readable form of written Gikuyu.

This short guide is designed to get you up to speed quickly with the modern Gikuyu language. We hope that after getting through it you will be able to read, write and speak basic Gikuyu sentences to express the following range of concepts:

1. I love you
2. Omari and Abdi are boys
3. John came here before I did
4. Who is that?
5. Amina will come home tomorrow
6. I came, I saw, I conquered
7. They do not like that
8. How did they eat five pizzas in two hours?
9. The family has entered their new house
10. Stop eating and hurry up!

For teachers of Gikuyu, this guide should provide you a basic outline for getting your new language learners to master the basic structure of the Gikuyu language. **Modern Gikuyu** is a spelling system for Gikuyu that uses spaces to separate pronouns from verbs. It is the spelling system used in this book.

Some explanations

In the text, any text marked with * indicates ungrammatical usage. Bolded text can be looked up in the index. The guide attempts to use plain English the first time a concept is explained; in this case the technical term is included in square brackets.

Pronunciations are surrounded by /.../ signs.

Written form   a

Spoken form   /a/

English translations are placed in italics in [ ] near their Gikuyu renditions.

We hope that this guide will help open up the culture of the Gikuyu-speaking peoples all over the world to you.

Reading Gikuyu

The easiest way to learn the rules [**grammar**] of a language is to read text written in that language. This section will help you analyse Gikuyu texts to extract meaning from them.

Recognising letters

Gikuyu is written with 20 letters [**alphabet**] (1).

Recognising words

The main types of words--**parts of speech**--used in Gikuyu are those that represent persons, places, things or ideas--**nouns**, and actions--**verbs**.

Aa	Bb	Cc	Dd	Ee	Gg
Hh	Ii	Ĩĩ	Jj	Kk	Mm
Nn	Oo	Rr	Tt	Uu	Ũũ
Ww	Yy				

Table 1: Gikuyu alphabet

Nouns

The nouns in every language are unlimited. Everything that has a name is a noun. Nouns can be represented by a single word or a group of words. Languages grow by making up new nouns to represent new things.

There are two main types of Modern Gikuyu nouns:

> **person nouns**, and
>
> **regular nouns**.

Note that formal written Gikuyu often has up to 10 types of nouns!

Gikuyu nouns dictate a lot about how the other parts of speech in a sentence are written down. This behaviour is called **concord** because all the parts of speech must agree with each other in a grammatically correct sentence.

When there is just one item of the noun [**singular**] or the noun cannot be counted, you do not need to modify the spelling in any way. When there is more than one [**plural**] of the noun, the spelling is modified to indicate this.

Regular nouns and person nouns form their plurals differently.

Person nouns

Person nouns generally begin with **mũ** when referring to the singular person. When referring to the plural, **mũ** [/mo/] is replaced by **a** [/a/] at the beginning (**prefix**) of the person noun.

Where the singular begins with **ka**, it is replaced in the plural by **tũ**.

	Singular	Plural
Gikuyu	**mũ**tumia	**a**tumia
English	woman	women
Gikuyu	**mũ**thuri	**a**thuri
English	man	men
Gikuyu	**kai**rĩtu	**tũ**irĩtu
English	girl	girls
Gikuyu	**ka**hĩĩ	**tũ**hĩĩ
English	boy	boys

Table 2: Person nouns

Regular nouns

Regular nouns form plurals predictably depending on their meaning (**semantic class**).

Suggests	_Singular_	_Plural_
not a person	**mũ**	**mĩ**
	mũtĩ [tree]	mĩtĩ [trees]
	mũrango [door]	mĩrango [doors]
	mũkebe [tin]	mĩkebe [tins]
objects	gĩ	i
	gĩtĩ [chair]	itĩ [chairs]
	gĩkombe [cup]	ikombe [cups]
	gĩtanda [bed]	itanda [beds]
objects	r	ma
	ritho [eye]	maitho [eyes]

Table 3: Regular nouns and their meaning-based groups.

So if the singular starts with **mũ**, the plural is formed by changing **mũ** to

- **a** if a person, or
- **mĩ** if not a person.

If the singular starts with **gĩ**, the plural is formed by changing **gĩ** to **i**.

When in doubt, try with **mũ** as the singular prefix, and **ma** as the plural prefix for nouns.

Describe Nouns - Adjectives

The quality of a noun is described by **adjectives**. Adjectives are placed after the noun. For example,

nyũmba njerũ [<u>new</u> <u>house</u>].

Again, since the noun dictates the form of all the other parts of speech, there are also two main types of adjectives:

- **person adjectives**, and
- **regular adjectives**.

Each adjective used to describe a noun must agree with the noun. Adjectives take the same prefixes as nouns.

Person adjectives

When an adjective describes a singular person noun, **mũ** is attached in front of the adjective. In older texts, this may also be represented as **mw**.

When referring to a plural person noun, **a** is attached to the front of the adjective. In older texts, the **a** may not be present since in the spoken form it is hardly distinct from the next vowel in the adjective.

Regular adjectives

Regular adjectives form alliterations with the nouns they are describing.

As with nouns, when in doubt, try with **mũ** as the singular prefix, and **ma** as the plural prefix for adjectives.

	Singular	Plural
Swahili	mūtumia **mūerū**	atumia **aerū**
English	**new** wife	**new** wives
Swahili	mūiritū mūthaka	airitū **athaka**
English	**beautiful** lady	**beautiful** ladies
Swahili	mūrutani **mūūrū**	arutani **aūrū**
English	**bad** teacher	**bad** teachers

Table 4: Adjectives **erū**, **thaka**, and **ūrū** with person nouns.

mū	mĩ
mūrango **mūerū** [new door]	mĩrango **mĩerū** [new doors]
mūti **mūega** [good tree]	mĩti **mĩega** [good trees]

gĩ	nj
gĩtĩ **kĩerū** [new chair]	itĩ **njerū** [new chairs]
gĩtĩ **kĩega** [good chair]	itĩ **njega** [good chairs]

rĩ	ma
ritho **rĩerū** [new eye]	maitho **maerū** [new eyes]
rĩtho **rĩega** [good eye]	maitho **maega** [good eyes]

mū	ma
ūthiũ **mūerū** [new face]	mothiũ **maerū** [new faces]
ūthiũ **mūega** [good face	mothiũ **maega** [good faces]

Table 5: Adjectives **erū** and **ega** with regular nouns.

Determiners

Where there is an article, it is written after the noun.

- **definite articles**
  kairĩtu kau [*the* girl], **kahĩĩ kau** [*the* boy]
  kahĩĩ karĩa [*that* boy]

- **indefinite articles**
  kahĩĩ [*a* boy, or, boy]
  mũgima [*an* adult, or, *adult*]
  kahĩĩ o ũguo [*some* boy]

Pronouns

Happily, pronouns can stand in for any noun. Which means that if you don't know the name of something, point at it and use a pronoun to refer to it instead!

There are two main types--just like the nouns they refer to:

person pronouns, and

regular pronouns.

Person pronouns

Subject pronouns usually replace a person noun at the beginning of a sentence. All subject pronouns come before a verb. For example,

nĩ thiaga [*I go*].

In older texts, the pronoun is usually written together with the verb as **nĩ**thiaga.

nĩ	*I*	ndi	*not I*
nĩũ	*you*	ndũ	*not you*
nĩa	*she/he*	nda	*not she/not he*
nĩtũ	*we*	tũti	*not we*
nĩmũ	*you (plural)*	mũti	*not you (plural)*
nĩma	*they*	mati	*not they*

Table 6: Subject pronouns for person nouns

Object pronouns come right before the verb when used. Object pronouns, listed in Table 7, are also written alone. For example,

Nĩũ **nye** ndete [*(You **me** love*) You love **me***].

nĩa **nye** ndete	he loves **me**
nĩa **kwe** ndete	he loves **you**
nĩa **mwe** ndete	he loves **her**
nĩa **mwe** ndete	she loves **him**
nĩa **twe** ndete	he loves **us**
nĩa **mwe** ndete	he loves **you (plural)**
nĩa **me** ndete	he loves **them**

Table 7: Object pronouns for person nouns.

Regular pronouns

Regular pronouns behave similarly. But there are only two to remember: **it**, and **they/them**.

They are placed right before the verb whenever they are used. Look at this example involving **gũthoma [to read]**

> Ibuku rĩrĩ. Nĩ-ndĩ-**rĩ**-thomete
> [*This book. I have read it*].

> Mabuku maya. Nĩ-ndĩ-**ma**-thomete
> [*These books. I have read them*]

Interrogative pronouns, listed in Table 8, are used to ask questions.

Gikuyu	English
nũ	who
nĩkĩ	what
nĩkĩ gĩtũmi	why
kũ	where
atĩa	how
ĩrĩkũ	which

Table 8: Interrogative pronouns.

Verbs

Remember to ask yourself whenever you see a Gikuyu verb:

- what is the indication of the period of time in which the action took place [**tense**]?,

The Infinitive - Describe the verb's action

In English, the infinitive is indicated by **to** placed before the verb. In Gikuyu, it is either **kũ**, or **gũ** if the verb starts with **c, k, t, th** or a vowel.

Gikuyu	English
gũ-ika	to do
gũ-kua	to die
gũ-thoma	to read
kũ-geithia	to greet
kũ-ria	to eat

Table 9: Infinitive verbs

Present Habitual - Action takes place habitually

This is for actions that take place on a regular basis [**habitual tense**]. Note that this tense doesn't use special pronouns.

Gikuyu	Literal English
nĩĩ nĩ thoma**ga**	Me, I read **habitually**
Amina nĩa thoma**ga**	Amina, she reads **habitually**

Table 10: Simple present habitual tense.

Present Continuous - Action is taking place

This is for an action in the process of taking place. It is indicated with **ra** in front of the verb.

Gikuyu	Literal English
nĩ **ra**thoma	I **am** read**ing**
Amina nĩa **ra**thoma	Amina, she **is** read**ing**

Table 11: Simple present continuous tense.

Past - Action took place in the past

The simple past is indicated by adding **ra** to the front of the verb AND replacing the **a** at the end of the verb with **ire**.

Gikuyu	Literal English
nĩ **ra**thek**ire**	I cook**ed**
Amina nĩa **ra**thek**ire**	Amina, she cook**ed**

Table 12: Past simple tense.

Future - Action will take place

The future tense is indicated by inserting the Gikuyu for *will* in front of the verb. *will* is indicated by **ka** or **ga** if the verb starts with **c, k, t, th** or a vowel.

Gikuyu	Literal English
nĩ **ga**thoma	I **will** read
Amina nĩa **ga**thoma	Amina, she **will** read
nĩ **ka**ria	I **will** eat
Amina nĩa **ka**ria	Amina, she **will** eat

Table 13: Future simple tense.

Describe Verbs - Adverbs

Adverbs describe the intensity of an action.
Like **adjectives**, **adverbs** are also placed after the verb. For example,

we nĩũ rĩaga **ihenya** [*you, you eat **quickly***].

Recognising sentences

There are three main sentence patterns you can use to communicate with others:

- making a statement [**declarative sentences**]
- asking a question [**interrogative sentences**]
- commanding [**imperative sentences**]

Making a statement

e.g. *I love you.*

Gikuyu Word Order	ni	kwe	ndete
Grammar	[Noun]	[Noun]	[Verb]
	required	*optional*	*required*
Literally*	I	you	love

So in the negative, *I do not love you* will follow the same pattern:

Gikuyu Word Order	ndi	kwe	ndete
Grammar	[Noun]	[Noun]	[Verb]
	required	*optional*	*required*
Literally*	not I	you	love

Asking a question

e.g. *Where are you going?*

Gikuyu Word Order	Wa	thĩĩ	kũ?
Grammar	[Noun]	[Verb]	[Interrogative pronoun]
	required	*required*	*required*
Literally*	You	go	where?

Commanding

e.g. *Stop making noise!*

Gikuyu Word Order	Tiga	kũnegena!
Grammar	[Verb]	[Noun]
	required	*optional*
Literally*	Stop	making noise!

Forming complex sentences

Conjunctions allow you to combine two or more similar components. These components may be two or more. For example, two nouns, or, three verbs, or five sentences.
Some common conjunctions are listed in Table 14.

Gikuyu	Omari **na** Abdi	rĩai **na mũcoke** mũkome
English	Omari **and** Abdi	eat **and then** sleep
Gikuyu	Omari **kana** Abdi	nĩakomete **kwoguo** koma
English	Omari **or** Abdi	I am sleeping **so** sleep
Gikuyu	**Akorwo** Amina ...	**Akorwo** Amina nĩagũka **nawe**, ...
English	**If** Amina ...	**If** Amina comes **then** ...
Gikuyu	**Ngĩ** ...	**Ona ndakorwo** ngomete ...
English	**While, When** I ...	**Even if** I sleep ...

Table 14: Common conjunctions.

Prepositions on the other hand are placed after nouns to indicate the position of some other noun. Table 15 lists some common prepositions.

Gikuyu	nĩ **ta** fufu	**ta ũrĩa** Buliva aroigire
English	it is **like** fufu	**as** Buliva said
Gikuyu	thĩĩ **ni**	thĩĩ **thĩ**
English	go **in**	go **down**
Gikuyu	thĩĩ **mbere ya** Amina oke	thĩĩ **ume** haha
English	go **before** Amina comes	go **from** here
Gikuyu	ũka **hakuhĩ** nanĩĩ	thĩĩ **thutha**
English	come **near** me	go **behind**

Table 15: Common prepositions.

The following sentence patterns therefore become easy to understand:

Omari a-rathĩĩ cukuru
[*Omari, he-go school
   (Omari is going to school)]

Omari na Abdi ma-rathĩĩ cukuru
[*Omari and Abdi, they-go school
   (Omari and Abdi are going to school)]

Omari na Abdi wa nĩma-komete mbere ya ma-thĩĩ cukuru
[*Omari and Abdi, they are sleeping before they go school
(Omari and Abdi are sleeping before they go to school)]

How to use a dictionary

Entries are listed first in order of appearance of their first letter. If the first letters are the same, they are further listed in order of appearance of their second letter. If the second letters are the same, they are further listed in order of appearance of their third letter. And so on.

Nouns are listed in the singular form. **kahĩĩ** [boy]

Verbs are listed in their positive form without the infinitive prefix. **thoma** [read]

Adjectives are listed without any indicator of noun agreement. **erũ** [new]

GIKUYU-ENGLISH

A, a

a lend (v)
  mpa iuku riri lend me this book
aciari parents (n)
  aciari bawe his parents
Afrika Africa (n)
  Cera Afrika visit Africa
aga bata disgrace (v)
  ugwe ni uku aga bata yakku you are disgracing yourself
ageni foreigner (n)
  ageni bagukinya the foreigners have arrived
ai ouch (excl)
  ai! irina murimo Ouch! It hurts
aka build (v)
  aka nyomba build a house
aki just (adj)
  ni waa aki it is just folly
amba paste (v)
  amba ruthingone to paste it on the wall
ambiiria begin (v)
  ambiiria kuria start eating
anda plant (v)
  anda muti to plant a tree

antu humankind (n)
  turi antu we are humankind
antu banaana eight persons (n)
  antu banaana ibeejite eight persons are coming
antu betu in-law (n)
  antu betu our in-laws
antu kenda nine persons (n)
  antu kenda nibejite nine persons are coming
ari no (excl)
  nkuga ari I say no
ariiria bargain (v)
  ariiria uguri bargain over price
aritwa student (n)
  aritwa mirongo iri twenty students
atha govern (v)
  atha Ghana govern Ghana
athaki cast (n)
  athaki ba sinema cast of a film
athukira branch (v)
  athukira aja branch here
atia how (adv)
  urigua atia? how does it feel?
au just (prep)
  Oriria akinyire au just as he got

1

there

B, b

baba these (p)
antu baba bareja these people came

babaingi several (adj)
antu babaingi ibeejire several people came

baisikili bicycle (n)
baisikili injeru new bicycle

baita profit (n)
thithia baita make profit

bajuuju batene ancestor (n)
bajuuju batene bakwa my ancestors

banga plan (v)
kiongo kimwe gitibangaga one head does not plan

banga arrange (v)
banga iti arrange the chairs

bathurumu lavatory (n)
ita bathurumu go to the lavatory

batithia baptise (v)
batithia John baptise John

bendera flag (n)
bendera ya yeluu yellow flag

bionthe all (det)
into bionthe all things

bionthe everything (p)
bionthe biguita bwega everything has gone well

bisi fees (n)
bisi ya cukuru school fees

bongwa themselves (p)
bagucimenyeera bongwa they look after themselves well

bonthe everyone (p)
bonthe bakeeja everyone will come

bonthe each and everyone (p)
bonthe bareeja each and everyone came

bubuega clearly (adv)
niukumiona bubuega you see it clearly

buuruka fly (v)
buuruka iguru matuune to fly into the sky

bwega very (adv)
ukuthithia bwega you have done very well

bwega clearly (adv)
niukumiona bwega you see it clearly

C, c

canura comb (v)
tumira gucanuri gucanura nchiuri ciaku use a comb to comb your hair

cenca march (v)
asikari ni bagucenca the soldiers are marching

cerithiria delay (v)
ugucerithiria you have delayed

chai tea (n)
chai iri na murio the tea is sweet

chenji change (n)
  wina chenji do you have change?
cia for (prep)
  cia bautwi for ourselves
cibitari hospital (n)
  ita cibitari go to a hospital
cimiti cement (n)
  maiga na cimiti stones and cement
ciothe all (det)
  Indo ciothe all things
cukuru school (n)
  a place where learning happens
  I learn to read at school
cuna lick (v)
  kuru ni igucuna kironda kiayo the dog is licking its sore
cunca kiss (v)
  cunca miromo yakwa kiss my lips

cuncha embrace (v)
  ncuncha embrace me
cuuba bottle (n)
  cuuba ithano five bottles
cuuma metal (n)
  nkobia ya cuuma hat of metal
cuuria hang (v)
  cuuria au hang it there
cwaa look for (v)
  cwaa maana to look for meaning

D, d

daawa medicine (n)
  daawa iri na ngana bitter medicine

dakinga second (n)
  ndakinga ikumi ten seconds

E, e

egera clear (v)
  egera mimero clear your throat
ejana donate (v)
  ejana kiri bo let us donate to them

enda love (v)
  ni nkwendete I love you
enketha belch (v)
  ria indi enketha eat then belch
ereithia explain (v)
  mbereithia explain to me
eruka melt (v)
  maguta ni ja kueruka the she-abutter is melting

F, f

famili family (n)
  famili injeru new family
freshi fresh (adj)
  mathangu freshi fresh leaves

G, g

ga let (v)
  ga twaambire gikundi let us found a group
Gacicia June (n)
  June has 30 days

gaciu knife (n)
noora gaciu sharpen a knife

gamba bark (v)
kuru ni iku-gamba a dog barks

garuka change (v)
igita riagaruka, garuka na igi-ita if time changes, change with the times

gatagatĩ-inĩ ka amongst (prep)
Gatagatĩ-inĩ ka andũ amongst people

gatigati amongst (prep)
gatigati ga antu amongst people

gatigati middle (adj)
kara gatigati be in the middle

gatu ga gwikira matu earpiece (n)
gantu gakeru gagwikira matu new earpiece

Gatumu December (n)
December has 31 days

gia give birth (v)
gia twana twa maatha to give birth to twins

gia iu be pregnant (v)
nkugia iu I am pregnant

gichanuri comb (n)
tumira gichanuri guchanura nchiuri use a comb to comb your hair

Gicunku English (n)
Mbaragia Gicunku I speak English

giempe drum (n)
inkuigua iempe I hear the drums

giita cut (v)
giita keki maita jairi to cut the cake in two

gikaro habitat (n)
gikaro kia nyomoo habitat of animals

gikeno happiness (n)
gikeno gigukinya happiness has arrived

gikiega good (adj)
kiewa gikiega a good gift

gikinya heel (n)
kiara gia kuguru na gikinya toe and heel

gikombe cup (n)
gikombe gia chai tea cup

gikonyo snail (n)
ni ndijaga gikonyo I eat snails

gikumenyeka distinguished (adj)
kiura gikumenyeka a distinguished frog

gikundi group (n)
twambirie gikundi let us found a group

gikundi grove (n)
gikundi kia miti grove of spirits

gikuyu fish (n)
gikuyu gikarangi fried fish

gikuyu fish (v)
twite tukagwatie gikuyu let's go and fish

gintu thing (n)
gintu, into the thing; the things

gintu gia kumamiria mutwe pillow (n)

gintu gia kumamiria mutwe na gitanda *pillow and bed*

gitambaa cloth (n)
ikira gitambaa wear cloth

gitambaa fabric (n)
ngurira gitambaa buy fabric for me

gitambaa gia kiongo headgear (n)
oga gitambaa gia kiongo put on headgear

gitame garment (n)
ikira gitame wear a garment

gitanda bed (n)
Mama iguru ria gitanda sleep on the bed

gitaru boat (n)
gitaru gigitune red boat

Gĩthathanwa May (n)
May has 31 days

Gĩthũngũ English (n)
nĩnjaragia Gĩthũngũ I speak English

giti chair (n)
banga iti arrange the chairs

gituma noise (n)
tiga kuringa gituma stop making noise

gitumi reason (n)
untu bunthe buri na gitumi everything has a reason

guaa ndene fall into (v)
guaa ndene ya kirinya fall into a pit

guaa nthi fall down (v)
nkara ikuguaa nthi the egg has fallen down

guaiya frighten (v)
guaiya antu babathuku frighten evil people

guciata fast (v)
guciata na kuromba fast and pray

gucienda selfishness (n)
gucienda guti thongi selfishness is not good

guciendithia befriend (v)
guciendithia uni befriend me

gucindwa defeat (n)
ushindi na gucindwa victory and defeat

guciumia determination (n)
tutakithia na guciumia we will do it with determination

gukaatha exultation (n)
ndwimbo cia gukaatha songs of exultation

gukara bwega prosperity (n)
thiiri na gukara bwega peace and prosperity

gũkenania amusing (adj)
Rũgano rwa gũkenania amusing story

gukenia entertaining (adj)
ni i gukenia it is entertaining

gukia daybreak (n)
gukia na muundu kuingira daybreak and nightfall

gukima pound (v)
gukima fufu I pound fufu

gukira fear (v)
gukira irundu bia akuu fear an

apparition

gukua die (v)
gukua urimuniini itindene *to die young in the play*

gukua crawl (v)
mwana niagukua *the child is crawling*

gukura grow (v)
mwana agukura *the child has grown*

gukura mono overgrow (v)
nyunjuri igukura mono *the backyard is overgrown*

guntanga bother (v)
ugwe ni uguntanga *you are bothering me*

guntu place (n)
guntu kuriku? *which place?*

gura buy (v)
gura gintu *to buy something*

gura marry (v)
ngura *marry me*

gusumbura bother (n)
gusumbura mono *too much bother*

guta gossip (v)
kumuguta *gossip about her*

gutanga bother (n)
gutanga gukuingi *too much bother*

gūtaranĩria addition (n)
1 +1=2; gũkũ nĩ gũtaranĩria *1 + 1 = 2; this is addition*

guteta argue (v)
guteta nawe *argue with him*

gutethani generosity (n)
gutethania gwaku *your generosity*

gutikio nothing (n)
gutikio ndinakio *I have nothing*

gutu ear (n)
gutu na nyuiuru *ear and nose*

gutumiiria proclamation (n)
gutumiiria uhuru bwa umuntu *proclamation of the rights of humankind*

guturikana overturn (v)
karai gaguturikana *the pan has overturned*

gwakana blazing (adj)
mwanki ju gwakana *blazing fire*

gwata catch (v)
gwata mubira *catch the ball*

gwata hold (v)
gwata njara yakwa *hold my hand*

gwatia kindle (v)
gwatia mwanki *kindle a fire*

gwatithania attach (v)
gwatithania na ruthingo *attach to wall*

gwenketha hiccups (n)
nia a gwenketha *he has got the hiccups*

gwitikia doubt (n)
ati gwitikia *she has doubts*

gwitura leak (v)
mutungi juju ni jugwitura *the bucket leaks*

I, i

i njiru   black (adj)
  nguo i njiru black cloth
i njumo   dry (adj)
  nthi i njumo dry land
i nkuru   old (adj)
  pani i nkuru old pan
i nthongi   beautiful (adj)
  ni i nthongi it is beautiful
ibuku   book (n)
  this book
icokio   answer (v)
  mpa icokio answer me
icungwa   orange (adj)
  ikira kobia ya rangi ya icungwa
  wear the orange cap
iembe   mango (n)
  iembe rikuguunda the mango has
  ripened
iembe   mango (n)
  iembe rikugunda the mango has
  ripened
igiita   moment (n)
  igiita rikuthira the moment is up
igita   period (n)
  imwe gaturumo ithano ni imwe
  na nusu 1.5 is one and a half.
igo   tooth (n)
  thambia maigo jaku brush your
  teeth
igoro   yesterday (adv)
  arakinyire igoro she arrived yes-
  terday
igoti   court (n)
  mbitite igotine I am going to court

igua ruriitho   be jealous (v)
  igua ruriitho iguru ria mukuru
  wawe be jealous over her husband

iguru   sky (n)
  huuruka wite iguru to fly into the
  sky
iguru   on (prep)
  mama iguru ria metha sleep on
  the table
iguru   up (adv)
  tega iguru look up
igwe mpio   cool (v)
  tiga igwe mpio let it cool
ija   come (v)
  kuija aja to come here
ijiri   two (adj)
  kuri na cuuba ijiri ruthingone
  There are two bottles on the wall
ikia miruki   breathe (v)
  ikia   miruki   aniini;   nogoka
  breathe a little; take a breather
ikira kiongo   memorize (v)
  gwikira kiongo to memorize
ikumi na imwe   eleven (adj)
  cuuba ikumi na imwe eleven bot-
  tles
ikumi na inyanya   eighteen
  (adj)
  cuuba ikumi na inyanya eighteen
  bottles
ikumi na ithano   fifteen (adj)
  cuuba ikumi na ithano fifteen
  bottles
imenyithia   news (n)
  imenyithia bia mauntu news of

the realm

imitune red (adj)
miromo imitune red lips

imwe one (adj)
kuri na cuuba imwe irungamire iguru ria nyomba There is one bottle standing on top of the house

indaaja long (adj)
kireru gikiraaja long beard

indi but (conj)
i nkumienda, indi I like it, but

indigo indigo (adj)
nguo ya indigo indigo cloth

inga chase (v)
gutiwe umwingatite no one is chasing him

inga close (v)
kuinga mulango to close the door

ingia increase (v)
wamba bukuingia burglary is increasing

ingura aniini prop (v)
ingura murango aniini prop the door

ing`ana how much (adj)
ing`ana atia? how much is it?

inja dig (v)
inja irinya to dig a hole

injeru new (adj)
famili injeru new family

injumo parched (adj)
ngozi injumo parched skin

inkuru outdated (adj)
lori inkuru outdated lorry

inthuku bad (adj)
kuru inthuku bad dog

inya effort (n)
inya injega a good effort

inya press (v)
iinya maita mugwanja to press it seven times

inya power (n)
inya na unene strength and power

inya four (adj)
The number 4 *kuri na cuuba inya ruthingone There are four bottles on the wall*

inyanya eight (adj)
cuuba inyanya eight bottles

inyia fine (adj)
thia inye buru grind it finely

inyiiria oppress (v)
ni ugumpinyiiria you are oppressing me

irandu debt (n)
ena marandu ja maingi he has many debts

irandu owe (v)
ndina irandu riaku I owe you

iri na utheri bright (adj)
nyomba iri na utheri bright room

irigiritwe na iria island (n)
Sezchelles irigiritwe na iria Seychelles island

irigu banana (n)
iruki niliendete irigu a monkey likes bananas

irigu plantain (n)
irigu na mukwacii plantain and cassava

irinda dress (n)
irinda ria mbuluu blue dress

irinya pit (n)
inja irinya dig a pit

irinya hoe (n)
irinya hoe and cutlass

irinya hole (n)
irinya riniini small hole

irio food (n)
ria irio eat food

iromba prayer (n)
iromba ni ririthongi prayer is good

iru knee (n)
maru jakwa my knees

iruki monkey (n)
iruki riendete marigu a monkey likes bananas

irundu bia akuu apparition (n)
gukira irundu bia akuu fear an apparition

irundu bibithuku ghost (n)
ndiona irundu bibithuku I see a ghost

Isilamu Islam (n)
Ukristu na Uisilamu Christianity and Islam

ita go (v)
gwita cukuru to go to school

ita call (v)
ita kaiji to call the boy

ita kioro go to the toilet (v)
gwita kioro o kiumia to go to the toilet weekly

ita mbere proceed (v)
ita mbere kuona he proceeded to see

itanambere continue (v)
itanambere na ngugi continue the work

ithaa hour (n)
mathaa ikumi ten hours

ithangu leaf (n)
ithangu ria ngirini green leaf

ithano five (adj)
The number 5 *cuuba ithano Five bottles*

ithanthatu six (adj)
cuuba ithanthatu six bottles

itharimo blessing (n)
Itharimo bia murungu God's blessing

ithe father (n)
ithe wa mwana waka ni muntu wetu my father's child is my sibling

ithia burn (v)
ithia maratasi jonthe burn all the papers

ithikira grieve (v)
nkoro yaka ni ikuithikira my soul grieves

ithori tear (n)
meetho jakwa jojurite maithori my eyes filled with tears

itia be wrong (v)
ndina maitia? am I wrong?

itikia believe (v)
itikia Kofi believe Kofi

itikiira allow (v)
Kubaitikiira allow them

itikiiria   accept (v)
ku mwitikiiria accept her
itinda   play (n)
tega itinda watch a play
itithia   drive (v)
gwitithia ngari drive a car
itumbi ria munda   garden egg (n)
gitwero kia itumbi ria munda garden egg stew
itumo   spear (n)
bamumuntire na itumo they pierced him with a spear
ituu   cloud (v)
iguru rikugia ituu the sky has clouded
ituu   cloud (n)
ituu ri rieru a white cloud
ituura   pour (v)
ituura ruuji pour water
iu   that (p)
nyoni iu that bird
iu   it (p)
iu ni iguaga it falls
iua   flower (n)
iua ririthongi pretty flower
iuku   book (n)
iuku riri this book
iuti   boil (n)
iuti riri murimo a boil is painful

J, j

jama   jama (n)
ina jama sing jama

jollof   jollof (n)
jollof ni irio jollof is food
jukia   pick up (v)
jukia maiga pick up the stones
Jumamosi   Saturday (n)
Twana twa muthenya jwa Jumamosi Saturday children
Jumatatũ   Monday (n)
ciana cia Jumatatũ Monday children

K, k

kaari ka mwariocia   niece (n)
aari ba mwariocia my nieces
kaatha   commend (v)
kumukaatha commend her
kabati ga kwojera mati   dustpan (n)
kiegeri na kabati ga kwojera mati broom and dustpan
kagiita gakoomo   dry season (n)
kagiita gakoomo gagukinya the dry season has arrived
kaiji   boy (n)
Kaiji kari aja the boy is here
kaingi   often (adv)
ejaga aja kaingi she often comes here
kairi   again (adv)
kumwona kairi see her again
kaja   outside (n)
ita kaja go outside
kajau   calf (n)
Kajau kawe ni gakathongi her calves are beautiful

kajea dove (n)
kajea gakeeru white dove
kameme radio (n)
ingurira kameme switch on the radio
kamera camera (n)
gicicio gia kamera lens of a camera
kamindo cutlass (n)
neekeria kamindo give me the cutlass
Kamũgaa September (n)
September has 30 days
kana or (conj)
Kofi kana Ama Kofi or Ama
kana ka ngurwe piglet (n)
twana twa ngurwe piglets
kania forbid (v)
kania we forbid her
kanisa church (n)
ita kanisa go to church
Kanyua Hũngũ November (n)
November has 30 days
kaora slowly (adv)
nkuru itaga kaora a tortoise walks slowly
karai pan (n)
karai gagakuru old pan
karamu pen (n)
rangi ya karamu ink in a pen
karamu ka mata pencil (n)
maguta kiri karamu ka mata grease in a pencil
karanga fry (v)
tumira maguta ja mboga gukaranga gikuyu use vegetable

oil to fry fish
karatasi page (n)
ingura karatasi ga mirongo iiri open page twenty-two
kathia deer (n)
simba niyendete nyama ya kathia a lion likes deer meat
kauna waist (n)
kauna gaku your waist
kauna bodice (n)
ekagira nguu ya kauna she wears a bodice
kayamba castanet (n)
inithia kayamba play the castanets
kebab khebab (n)
kebab na ncobi khebabs and beer
kenya na kenya forever (adv)
aturaga kenya na kenya she lives forever
kethia greet (v)
Kethia Ama greet Ama
kethira if (conj)
kethira ni a kwendete if someone loves you
kia fool (n)
Kia!! Kia! Fool! Dimwit!
kiao leniency (n)
mwigirue kiao show him leniency

kiao empathy (n)
ari na kiao she has such empathy
kiara finger (n)
mbonia kiara giaku show me your finger

kiara gia kuguru toe (n)
kiara gia kuguru na gikinya toe
and heel

kiatho event (n)
kiatho gikuambiriria the event
has started

kiatho party (n)
mbitite kiatho I am going to a
party

kiatho event (n)
kiatho gikwambiria the event has
started

kibara chest (n)
nchiuri cia kibara chest hair

kibodi keyboard (n)
iinya k kiri kibodi press k on the
keyboard

kiegeri broom (n)
*kiegeri na kabati ga kwojera
mati* broom and dustpan

kiewa award (n)
mue kiewa give her an award

kiewa gift (n)
kiewa gikiega a good gift

kigeranio exam (n)
kigeranio gikiuthu the exam is
easy

kigimbi goosebumps (n)
ndina kigimbi I have got goosebumps

kigongoana sacrifice (n)
rita kigongoana offer a sacrifice

kĩhoti-othe almighty (adj)
Ngai kĩhoti-othe almighty god

Kĩhu March (n)
March has 31 days

Kĩhu gĩa Kerĩ October (n)
October has 31 days

kiimba corpse (n)
kiimba igukora the corpse is rot-
ting

kilomita kilometer (n)
kilomita ikumi ten kilometers

kilomita kilometre (n)
kilomita ikumi ten kilometres

kimenyano favoritism (n)
tiga kimenyano stop the favoritism

kimera plant (n)
kimera gigitune red plant

kingangiri crab (n)
subu ya kingangiri crab soup

kingangiri crocodile (n)
*kingangiri kiendete gukara ruu-
jine* a crocodile likes water

kingotore coin (n)
ingotore bina four coins

kinya arrive (v)
wakinya undingire thimu when
you arrive, call me

kinyiiria force (v)
ugwe ga ugunkinyiiria you are
forcing me

kiondo bag (n)
tega kiondo look at the bag

kiongo mind (n)
kiongo kiawe her mind

kiongo head (n)
kiongo gikinene your big head

kiongone heading (n)
kiongone kia iuku book headings

kioni mirror (n)
kioni gikinene big mirror
kira quiet (adj)
kira kii be quiet
kiragutia butterfly (n)
kiragutia gikithongi a butterfly is beautiful
kiratasi paper (n)
kiratasi kia narua today's paper
kiratu shoe (n)
footwear that covers all of the foot *ikira iratu biaku wear your shoes*
kireru beard (n)
kireru gikinene long beard
kirima hill (n)
kirima iguru hill top
kirima mountain (n)
kirima iguru mountain peak
kirindi crowd (n)
kirindi kiri na gituma noisy crowd
kiroria prophet (n)
kiroria wama powerful prophet
kithao inactive (n)
ni kithao he is inactive
kitheti basket (n)
Kamata kitheti carry a basket
kithomo reading (n)
cookera kithomo repeat the reading
kithomo education (n)
ugima bwa mwiri na kithomo health and education
kiu stomach (n)
kiu gikinene big stomach

kiu abdomen (n)
Kiu gia kuru abdomen of a dog
kiugu coop (n)
kiugu kia nguku hen coop
kiumia service (n)
kiumia gia gucokia nkaatho thanksgiving service
Kiumia Sunday (n)
Kwasi na Akosua nĩ ciana cia Kiumia Kwasi and Akosua are Sunday children
kiura frog (n)
kiura kiendete ruuji a frog likes water
kiuria question (n)
ndina kiuria I have a question
kobithia loan (v)
nkobithia mbeca loan me money
kochi coach (n)
kochi ya timu ya mubira jwa maguru a football team coach
kokoa cocoa (n)
muti jwa kokoa cocoa tree
kona corners (n)
kona cionthe cia nthiguru all corners of the world
korora cough (v)
korora nainya to cough profusely
koti court (n)
Mbitite kotini I am going to court
kuandanira falsification (n)
kwaria urongo na kuandanira lies and falsifications
kuaririria preface (n)
kuaririria iuku book preface

kuetheria pretend (v)
ni ukuetheria you are pretending
kugaa division (n)
ijiri kugaira imwe ni ijiri ; guku ni kugaa 2/1 = 2; this is division
kũgegania amazing (adj)
Rũgano rwa kũgegania amazing story
kugegania amusing (adj)
rugono rwa kugegania amusing story
kugia gain (v)
kethira ndi mwoyo, ni ninkugia gintu kionthe if I have life, I have gained everything
kugia matunda bear fruit (v)
muti jukugia matunda the tree has borne fruit
kugia mpio get wet (v)
guntu gukugia mpio the place has gotten wet
kugiana friction (n)
kugiana kurejira gatigati geetu friction came between us
kugitirwa igamba judgement (n)
Kugitirwa igamba ririku which judgement?
kugurana marriage (n)
kugurana gukuega good marriage

kuguru leg (n)
kuguru kuimbite swollen leg
kugwatagwata caress (v)
njara yawe ikugwatagwata her hand caresses it

kugwirirua appreciate (v)
ugwe utikugwirirua buu you do not appreciate this
kuigirua kiao pitiable (adj)
Kana gaka ni ga kuigirua kiao pitiable child
kuigithia bu bubuthuku disgusting (adj)
guntu kuu ni gu kuigithia bu bubuthuku the place is disgusting

kuigua bubui be ill (v)
ni nkuigua bubui I am ill
kuigua bui be guilty of (v)
ni tukuigua bui we are guilty
kuigua nthoni be shy (v)
ni nkuigua nthoni I am shy
kuina dance (v)
kuina na gikeno to dance with joy

kuinyiirua oppression (n)
Kuinyiirua!! such oppression!
kuithikira grief (n)
kuithikira ni gukumburaga grief is killing me
kuma carve (v)
kuma rubau carve the wood
kumemorise memorization (n)
kumemorise ni gukuthongi some memorization is good
kumenyeka become famous (v)
Nkrumah ni akumenyeka Nkrumah has become famous
kumenyerera protection (n)
mpa umenyereri give me protection

kumithia praise (v)
gukumithia Ngai to praise God
kumuntwa cindano injection (n)
kumuntwa cindano kuri murimo an injection is painful
kunga crow (v)
nchamba ni igukunga a cockerel is crowing
kungwata have a hold on (v)
Mpara ikungwata hunger has a hold on me (I am hungry)
kung`anana equal (adj)
twinthe gatung`anene we are equal
kunika cover (v)
kunika na nguo; ikira nguo cover with cloth; dress in cloth
kunikara overflow (v)
muuro jukunikara the lake has overflowed
kunja fold (v)
kunja nguo ya ngina to fold mother's cloth
kunja bend (v)
kunja aniini bend it a bit
kunthe everywhere (p)
kunthe kuri na mwanki everywhere is hot
kunya pinch (v)
tiga gunkunya stop pinching me
kunyanira betray (v)
ugankunyanira do not betray me
kunyua drink (v)
kunyua ruuji to drink water

kura pluck (v)
kura itunda pluck fruit
kũrakaria annoying (adj)
Nĩ wa kũrakaria harĩ we it is annoying to you
kuriganirua forgetfulness (n)
kuriganirua kwawe her forgetfulness
kurigarania amazing (adj)
rugono rwa kurigarania amazing story
kurio early (adv)
wije kurio come early
kurita deduct (v)
kurita imwe kuma kiri ijiri deduct one from two
kuriuka resurrection (n)
kuriuka gwa Kiristu the resurrection of Christ
kuroria prophesy (v)
kuroria kuendelea prophesy prosperity
kuru dog (n)
kuru nikugamba a dog barks
kurua battle (v)
twitite kurua nabo we are going to battle them
kuruka pass (v)
kethira ugakuruka undingire thimu if you are passing, call me
kuthaaka play (v)
gatukuthaaka we are playing
kuthera holy (adj)
iuku riritheru holy book
kuthinika suffering (n)
uguaa na kuthinika fear with suf-

fering

kuthira miruki deflate (v)
tairi yaku ikuthira miruki your tyre is deflating

kuthiria annul (v)
kuthiria muranu annul a marriage

kuthuranira preparation (n)
thuranira make preparation

kuthuria annoying (adj)
ni i kuthuria it is annoying to you

kuuga mbuu wailing (n)
kurira na kuuga mbuu crying and wailing

kuugia mai fart (n)
mai jawe i ja kununka her fart smells badly

kuugithia mainda multiplication (n)
ijiri kuugithia mainda na imwe ni ijiri; guku ni kuugithia mainda 2 x 1 = 2; this is multiplication

kuuma from (prep)
ita kuuma aja go from here

kuuma tharike bleeding (n)
rigiria kuuma tharike stop the bleeding

kuumia dry (v)
kuumia nguo to dry clothes

kuumiria patience (n)
wendo na kuumiria love and patience

kuumiriria encouragement (n)
kuumiriria na gukena encour-

agement and joy

kuumiriria comfort (n)
mpa kuumiriria give me comfort

kuura peel off (v)
kuura yumba peel off the plaster

kuura disappear (v)
a kuura she has disappeared

kuura beat (v)
kuura muntu beat someone

kwaria urongo perjury (n)
kwaria urongo kotini perjury in court

kwenda need (v)
kwenda mucii to need family

kwenda desire (v)
inkwenda irigu I desire a banana

kwendeka desirable (adj)
ni i kwendeka it is desirable

kwendia hawk (v)
kwendia into hawk things

kwerenca plead with ... (v)
ndakwerenca; itu i plead with you; please

kwinaina kwa nthiguru earthquake (n)
nthiguru i kwinaina it is an earthquake

kwinyiha humility (n)
inyihe be humble

kwithirwa being (n)
kwithirwa na U muntu human being

kwombika by any chance (adv)
kwombika withirwa ukumwona have you seen her by any chance?

L, l

leki lake (n)
leki ikunikara the lake has over-flowed
logo logo (n)
logo ya kanisa church logo
lori lorry (n)
kirungamo kia lori lorry stop

M, m

macindano competition (n)
macindano ja mubira jwa maguru football competition
macokanĩrio argument (n)
Macokanĩrio maingĩ many arguments
maguka ma tene ancestor (n)
maguka makwa ma tene my ancestors
maguru ja ngurwe pigfeet (n)
cubu ya maguru ja ngurwe pigfeet soup
maguta ja naathi palm kernel oil (n)
maguta ja naathi ni jameega ja nciuri palm kernel oil is good for hair
maguta ja ngirisi grease (n)
maguta ja ngirisi jari karaine grease in a pan
maiga stone (n)
maiga na cimiti stones and cement

maili mile (n)
maili ikumi ten miles
maindi buttocks (n)
maindi ja manene big buttocks
makara charcoal (n)
nkuniu ya makara sack of charcoal
makathi scissors (n)
mpa makathi give me the scissors

makosa mistake (n)
muntu wonthe omba kuthithia makosa everyone makes mistakes
makunu mushroom (n)
subu ya makunu mushroom soup

mamba alligator (n)
mamba nĩrĩ mũting'oe an alligator has a tail
mami mother (n)
mwana wa mami ni wetu my mother's child is my sibling
mamira phlegm (n)
angura mamira wipe the phlegm
mamira lean on (v)
mamira lean on me
mandamu madam (n)
mandamu Mary madam Mary
manĩrĩra announcement (n)
Thoma manĩrĩra read the announcement
manyoya ja naathi palmnut wool (n)
manyoya ja naathi jaijaga bwega mono palmnut wool burns well

marakara anger (n)
Horeria marakara maku calm your anger

marii compensation (n)
ukwona marii jaku? have you received your compensation?

maromba prayer (n)
maromba i jamega prayer is good

mashindano competition (n)
mashindano ja mubira jwa maguru football competition

mashini machine (n)
mashini injeru new machine

Masindano ja micetho Olympics (n)
Masindano ja micetho Olympics competition

mataaro advice (n)
Mũbĩa nĩarĩ mataaro a priest has advice

mataro advice (n)
mutumiria ari na mataro a priest has advice

mateta argument (n)
mateta jamaingi many arguments

mathanduku drawers (n)
wikirite mathanduku are you wearing drawers?

mathangu ja kokoyamu cocoyam leaves (n)
gitwero kia mathangu ja kokoyamu cocoyam leaves stew

mathiko funeral (n)
mbitiite mathiko I am going to a funeral

mati junk (n)
kuri na mati nyomba iu there is junk in the room

matuka flee (v)
aramatuka he fled

mbaki tobacco (n)
nyua mbaki smoke tobacco

mbaluni balloon (n)
mbaluni ijiri two balloons

mbarathi horse (n)
mbarathi injeru white horse

mbea mouse (n)
mbea ineene a big mouse

mbea mouse (n)
mbea iinene a big mouse

mbeca money (n)
mbeca itethagia money helps

mbere in front (prep)
ita mbere go in front

mbere before (prep)
ria mbere ya umama eat before (you) sleep

mbere ya antu public (n)
*u tiumba kuuga '***' mbere ya antu* you don't say 'vagina' in public

mbia rat (n)
mbia inene a big rat

mbica photograph (n)
ringa mbica take a photograph

mbica picture (n)
mbica inthongi beautiful picture

mbluu blue (adj)
nguo ya rangi ya mbluu blue dress

mbogisi box (n)
mbogisi A ni inene kiri mbogisi B
box A is bigger than box B
mbui feather (n)
mbui cia nyoni bird's feathers
mbuibui spider (n)
nyomba ya mbuibui spider's web
mburi goat (n)
mburi na ngondu a goat and a
sheep
meethene living room (n)
tukarite nthi meethene we are sit-
ting in the living room
meethene living room (n)
tukarite nthii meethene we are
sitting in the living room
meetho lens (n)
meetho ja kamera lens of a camera

menya know (v)
ninkumumenya I know her
menyera protect (v)
menyera bautwi protect us
menyithia alert (v)
ku ba menyithia alert them
miromo lips (n)
miromo imitune red lips
mirongo inna duration (n)
igita ria mathaa mirongo inna
forty-hour duration
mirugu god (n)
mirungu ya kwithondekera de-
pendable god
miruki breath (n)
kuucia miruki; nogoka collect
your breath; rest

mita meter (n)
mita ikumi ten meters
mita metre (n)
length metric; meter (American
English) *mita ikumi ten metres*
mitugo manner (n)
mitugo yawe ni imithongi his
manner is amusing
mitugo habit (n)
mitugo imithuku bad habit
mitugo character (n)
mitugo yawe her character
mkulima farmer (n)
ni mkulima she is a farmer
mono very much (adv)
ibwega mono thank you very
much
mono too much (adv)
arumanaga mono he insults too
much
mpaka cat (n)
mpaka iri na muthirinya a cat
has a tail
mpaka cat (n)
mpaka iri na munyiritha a cat
has a tail
mpakuri collander (n)
tumira mpakuri kunyaria ruuji
mucherene use the collander to
drain the rice
mpara hunger (n)
mpara na nyonta hunger and
thirst
mpempe corn (n)
mpempe na ncugu karanga corn
and groundnuts

mpio   cold (adj)
ruuji ruri na mpio cold water
mpio   cold temperature (n)
utuku buri na mpio night is cold
muaandiki   journalist (n)
turi aandiki we are journalists
Mũafrika   African (n)
someone   from   Africa   *Ndĩ
Mũafrika I am an African*
muajie   patient (n)
*ajie bararaga aja the patients
sleep here*
mubira   ball (n)
thaka mubira play ball
mubira   pipe (n)
ruuji rwa mubira pipe water
mucemanio   meeting (n)
*kansa mucemanio cancel the
meeting*
mucetho   game (n)
thaka mucetho play a game
muchere   rice (n)
muchere na mboco rice and beans

mucibi   film (n)
thaka mucibi cast of a film
mucore   friend (n)
mucore wakwa my friend
mucore umwega   good friend
(n)
*turi acore babega sana we are
very good friends*
mucoriru   bud (v)
*mpempe ni ikuma mucoriru the
maize is budding*

mucumari   nail (n)
*mucumari na kimuti plank and
nail*
Mũgaa   January (n)
January has 31 days
mugambi   judge (n)
agambi mugwanja seven judges
mugambo   language (n)
migambo i mingi many languages

mugate   bread (n)
mugate jumworo soft bread
mugeka   mat (n)
*tamburukia mugeka spread out a
mat*
mugeka   mat (n)
tandika mugeka spread out a mat

mugeni   guest ()
uni ndi mugeni I am a guest
mugeni   guest (n)
ndi mugeni I am a guest
Mũgetho   February (n)
February has 28 or 29 days
mũgima   adult (n)
nĩ mũndũ mũgima he is an adult
Mũgiranjara   August (n)
August has 31 days
mugunye   shade (n)
*nkarite mugunyene I am sitting
under the shade*
mugurani   groom (n)
*mucore wa mugurani groom's
friends*
muguuta jwa ngombe   cowhide
(n)

waache na muguuta jwa ngombe *my husband*
waache and cowhide
mugwatia wa ikuyu fisherman
(n)
ni mugwatia wa ikuyu he is a fisherman
mugwongo ivory (n)
mukathi jwa mugwongo ivory necklace
muiki bride (n)
mukuru wa muiki; muikithania bride's husband; groom
muikithania groom (n)
acore ba muikithania groom's friends
mũini musician (n)
the musicians
mukarire disposition (n)
mukarire jwa muntu a person's disposition
mukathi gaudy (adj)
mukathi jukwonekana gaudy necklace
mukathi necklace (n)
Mukathi jwa mugwongo ivory necklace
mukawa hotel (n)
araraga mukawa ene she sleeps at a hotel
mukiristu Christian (n)
mukiristu na muisilamu a Christian and a Muslim
mukobo loan (n)
ikwenda mukobo I need a loan
mukuru husband (n)
impendete mukuru wakwa I love

mukuru elder (adj)
mwana wetu uria mukuru my elder sibling
mukuru umukuru old man (n)
Ni mukuru umukuru he is an old man
mukwacii cassava (n)
marigu na mukwacii plantain and cassava
mulango door (n)
inga mulango close the door
mumbi creator (n)
ngai mumbi creator god
mumero throat (n)
theria mumero clear your throat
munda land (n)
gura munda buy land
mundu dark (adj)
utuku buri na mundu dark night
mundu darkness (n)
utuku buretaga mundu night brings darkness
munene almighty (adj)
ngai munene almighty god
munene king (n)
ni munene he is a king
munene wa nthiguru president (n)
munene wa nthiguru agukinya the president has arrived
munta inject (v)
munta inject me
munthu enemy (n)
anthu bakanoga enemies will tire

muntu person (n)
muntu wa bata important person

muntu master (n)
Muntu Kofi Master Kofi

muntu mugima adult (n)
ni muntu mugima he is an adult

muntu muka woman (n)
muntu muka umuthongi a pretty woman

muntu murume gentleman (n)
muntu murume u munene senior gentleman

muntu utiumii dimwit (adj)
kiaa! muntu utiumii! Fool! Dimwit!

muntu wa gukamata mirigo porter (n)
muntu wa gukamata mirigo akamataga kibogisi the porter carries a box

muntu wa gutethia antu philanthropist (n)
we ni muntu wa gutethia antu she is a philanthropist

muntu wa kumama na aka ouu philanderer (n)
uciethetie muntu wa kumama na aka ouu you have made yourself a philanderer

muntu wetu relative (n)
ni muntu wetu he is a relative

munyanya concubine (n)
yaa ni munyanya wakwa Yaa is my concubine

Muoria Nyoni July (n)
July has 31 days

muragani murderer (n)
ni muragani he is a murderer

murashi jwa kuthambia maigo toothbrush (n)
murashi jwa kuthambia maigo na ndawa toothbrush and toothpaste

murigitathi nurse (n)
ni murigitathi she is a nurse

murimo sickness (n)
urina murimo juriku what sickness have you?

murimo disease (n)
oria murimo heal disease

muringiti blanket (n)
muringiti juri na ruuji wet blanket

murio sweet (adj)
chai iri na murio the tea is sweet

muriti wa ngugi maid (n)
ni muriti wa ngugi she is a maid

muromo mouth (n)
muromo jwakwa my mouth

murongo liar (n)
arongo bathatu three liars

murugi chieftain (n)
ni murugi she is a chieftain

muruki smell (n)
ni nkuigua muruki I sense a smell

muruki fragrance (n)
muruki juu ni jwa batta the fragrance of sheabutter

murururu lizard (n)
murururu jurijaga nyaki a lizard eats grass

musiki music (n)
ina musiki play music

musingi foundation (n)
musingi jwa nyomba foundation of the house

mutanocia brother (n)
mutanocia wakwa my only brother

Mūthaatū April (n)
April has 30 days

muthao lazy (adj)
muntu muthao lazy man

Muthenya jwa ina Thursday (n)
twana twa Muthenya jwa ina Thursday children

Muthenya jwa iri Tuesday (n)
Twana twa muthenya jwa iri Tuesday children

Muthenya jwa ithatu Wednesday (n)
twana twa Muthenya jwa ithatu Wednesday children

Muthenya jwa kiumia Sunday (n)
Kimathi na Nkirote baciarirwe Muthenya jwa kiumia Kwasi and Akosua are Sunday children

Muthenya jwa mwambirio jwa kiumia Monday (n)
twana twa Muthenya jwa mwambirio jwa kiumia Monday children

muthetu brown (adj)
nyoni ya rangi ya muthetu brown bird

muthetu ash (n)
makara na muthetu charcoal and ashes

muthetu jwa yumba clay (n)
Glasi ya muthetu jwa yumba clay vase

muthia end (n)
muthia jugukinya the end has come

muthikiri listener (n)
mugeni athikiri hello listeners

muthirinya tail (n)
mpaka iri na muthirinya a cat has a tail

muthirinya penis (n)
utiumba kuuga 'muthirinya' mbere ya antu you don't say 'penis' in public

muti jwa kiegeri broomstick (n)
miti ikumi ya biegeri ten broomsticks

muti jwa kuringa gitaru paddle (n)
gitaru na muti jwa kuringa gitaru canoe and paddle

mutongeria leader (n)
uju niwe mutongeria wetu this is our leader

mutumiiria priest (n)
mutumiiria ari na mataro a priest has advice

mutumiria bishop (n)
ni mutumiria she is a bishop

mutumwa messenger (n)
atumwa ibakinyire the messengers arrived
mutungi bucket (n)
mutungi juturiki the bucket leaks

mutungi barrel (n)
ujuria mutungi fill up the barrel
mutungi pail (n)
mutungi na thabuni pail and soap

mutungi jar (n)
mitungi mugwanja seven jars
muturiru flute (n)
rwimbo rwa muturiru flute music

mutuu flour (n)
mutuu jwa mpempe corn flour
mutwe headache (n)
mutheega jwa mutwe headache medicine

mutwe headache (n)
ndwa ya mutwe headache medicine
muubira elastic (adj)
murigi jwa muubira elastic string

muuko pocket (n)
gutikio kiri ndene ya muuko jwakwa nothing inside my pocket

muuma oath (n)
muuma jungwa great oath
muunda farm (n)
munda jwa cocoua cocoa farm

muundu kugwaa nightfall (n)
muthenya na muundu kugwaa daybreak and nightfall
muuragani murderer (n)
ni muuragani he is a murderer
muuri pestle (n)
muuri na ntiri pestle and mortar
mwaandiki writer (n)
uni ndi mwaandiki I am a writer
mwaburi umbrella (n)
kara nthii rungu rwa mwaburi sit under the umbrella
Mwafrica African (n)
Uuni ni Mwafrica I am an African

mwago luxury (n)
ndiona mwago uturone bwaku I see luxury in your future
mwaka year (n)
mwaka jumweru jugukinya a new year has come
mwalimu teacher (n)
uni ndi mwalimu I am a teacher
mwamba thief (n)
ti mwamba he is not a thief
mwana toddler (n)
mwana, inaa witite toddler, where are you going?
mwana child (n)
mwana wa mami ni muntu wetu my mother's child is my sibling
mwana baby (n)
ndina mwana I have a baby
mwananchi citizen (n)
Uni ni mwananchi I am a citizen

mwanki hot (adj)
ruuji ruri na mwanki hot water
mwanki fire (n)
gwatia mwanki light the fire
mwari damsel (n)
mwari uju nathongi this damsel is
pretty
mwari miss (n)
mwari na kaari kaniini lady and
young lady
mwari girl (n)
mwari umuraaja tall girl
mwario ng'ina sister (n)
mwario ng'ina wakwa wenka my
only sister
mwekuru wife (n)
*mwekuru wakwa na twana
twakwa* my wife and my children
mwekuru missus (n)
mwekuru wa Clinton Missus Clinton
mwekuru umukuru old lady (n)
mwekuru umukuru wakwa my
old lady
mwendwa wakwa beloved (n)
mwendwa wakwa agumpairia
my beloved has tricked me
mweri month (n)
mweri jumwe one month
mweri moon (n)
mweri na jota moon and stars
Mweri jwa ikumi October (n)
*Mweri jwa ikumi jwithagirwa na
ntuku mirongo ithatu na imwe*
October has 31 days

Mweri jwa ikumi na jumwe
November (n)
*Mweri jwa ikumi na jumwe
jwithagirwa na ntuku mirongo
ithatu* November has 30 days
Mweri jwa Ina April (n)
*Mweri jwa Ina jwithagirwa na
ntuku mirongo ithatu* April has 30
days
Mweri jwa inana August (n)
*Mweri jwa inana jwithagirwa na
ntuku mirongo ithatu na imwe*
August has 31 days
Mweri jwa iri February (n)
*Mweri jwa iri jwithagitwa na
ntuku mirongo iri na inana kana
mirongo iri na kenda* February
has 28 or 29 days
Mweri jwa itantatu June (n)
*Mweri jwa itantatu jwithagirwa
na ntuku mirongo ithatu* June has
30 days
Mweri jwa kenda September
(n)
*Mweri jwa kenda jwithagirwa na
ntuku mirongo ithatu* September
has 30 days
Mweri jwa mugwanja July (n)
*Mweri jwa mugwanja juitha-
girwa na ntuku mirongo ithatu
na imwe* July has 31 days
Mweri jwa mwambirio January
(n)
*Mweri jwa mwambirio juitha-
girwa na ntuku mirongo ithatu
na imwe* January has 31 days

mwiri flesh (n)
  mwiri na tharike flesh and blood
mwitu bush (n)
  ita mwitune go into the bush
mwoyo living (adj)
  Ngai uri mwoyo living god

N, n

na and (conj)
  Kofi na Ama Kofi and Ama
na and (conj)
  Kofi na Ama Kofi and Ama
nanasi pineapple (n)
  ruuji rwa nanasi pineapple juice
nanasi pineapple (n)
  juici ya nanasi pineapple juice
narua today (adv)
  agakinya narua she arrives today

nasi nurse (n)
  ni nasi she is a nurse
nau mbere future (n)
  ndiona maisha ja raha nau mbere I see luxury in your future
nceege porcupine (n)
  irinya ria nceege porcupine hole
nceera jail (n)
  ita nceera go to jail
nceera prison (n)
  ita nceera go to prison
nchana alligator (n)
  nchana iri na muthirinya an alligator has a tail
nchiuri hair (n)
  nchiuri cia kibara chest hair

ncini pepper (n)
  ncini ni ikuithia the pepper burns

nciuri cia riitho eyebrow (n)
  riitho na nciuri cia riitho eye and eyebrow
ncoobi liquor (n)
  ikira ncoobi niini pour a little liquor
ncugu groundnut (n)
  mpeme na ncugu corn and groundnuts
ncugu groundnut (n)
  mpempe na ncugu corn and groundnuts
ncuma metal (n)
  kobia ya ncuma hat of metal
nda abdomen (n)
  Nda ya ngui abdomen of a dog
ndagika minute (n)
  ndagika ithano five minutes
ndagitari doctor (n)
  ni ndagitari she is a doctor
ndawa medicine (n)
  ndawa iri na ng'ana bitter medicine
ndawa ya kuthambia maigo toothpaste (n)
  murashi na ndawa ya kuthambia maigo toothbrush and toothpaste
ndege aeroplane (n)
  ndege igĩrĩ two aeroplanes
ndege aeroplane (ṅ)
  ndege ijiri two aeroplanes

ndekera forgive (v)
*ndekera maitia jakwa forgive me
my wrong*

ndene inside (adv)
ita ndene go inside

ndene in (prep)
*iri ndene ya nyomba it is in the
house*

ndereba driver (n)
*ndereba aguikira breki the driver
has braked*

ndimu lime (n)
juici ya ndimu lime juice

ndirisha window (n)
*rugura ndirisha open the win-
dows*

ndito heavy (adj)
ni i ndito it is heavy

ndomba be able to (v)
*ndomba kuthuta muti I am able to
climb a tree*

ndua battle (n)
*twitite kiri ndua we are going to
battle*

ndua fight (v)
*Ali na Frayier ni bari na ndua Ali
and Frazier fought*

nduume mist (n)
nduume ya ruukiri morning mist

ndwaa battle (n)
*twitite ndwaaene we are going to
battle*

nene great (adj)
ritwa ri ri nene a great name

nene big (adj)
Adae u mu-nene Big Adae

ng'ondu sheep (n)
*nyama ya ng'ondu sheep meat (i.e.
mutton)*

ng'ana bitter (adj)
*ndawa iri na ng'ana bitter
medicine*

ngaloni gallon (n)
ngaloni ya ruuji a gallon of water

nganira befit (v)
ni bugukunganira it befits you

ngara bruise (v)
*waringa rwagi na muthuro wan-
gara kironda giaku you swat the
fly in anger and you bruise your
wound*

ngaranji garage (n)
ngaranji ya ngari car garage

ngari car (n)
itithia ngari drive a car

ngari car (n)
ngari twiw kaar

ngatunyi lion (n)
*ngatunyi irijaga nyama a lion
eats flesh*

ngecere bow-legged (adj)
*muntu murume uri na ngecere
bow-legged man*

ngii fly (n)
ngii niburukaga a fly flies

ngii blowfly (n)
*ngii ni ithuragia mono blowflies
are annoying*

ngii housefly (n)
ngii yomba gukamata mirimo a housefly can carry disease

ngoga miserly (adj)
ari na ngoga he is miserly

ngombe cow (n)
nyama yangombe cow meat; beef

ngong ngong gong gong (n)
thaka ngong ngong play the gong gong

ngorogoro storm (n)
ngorogoro na nkwa storm with thunder

nguo attire (n)
nguo yaku ni inthongi mono your attire is beautiful

nguo clothes (n)
gura nguo buy clothes

ngurwe pig (n)
ngurwe imwe ni cia pinki some pigs are pink

ngutu gossip (n)
ngutu ti injega gossip is not good

ngutu gossip (n)
ngutu ti inthongi gossip is not good

ngwataniro association (n)
ija ngwatanirone ya arume ya gutirimana come to the men's association meeting

niĩ I (p)
niĩndĩaga I eat

niini little (n)
ikira ncoobi niini pour a little liquor

niki why (adv)
niki uu? why so?

ningwa myself (p)
ni nciendete ningwa I love myself

niuntu because (conj)
niuntu ni nkwendete because I like you

niuntu buu in that case (adv)
niuntu buu ija in that case come

njaa home (n)
njaa yenu your home

njara arm (n)
ukiria njara yaku lift up your arm

njara hand (n)
ukiria njara yaku lift up your hand

njira way (n)
njira the way

njogu elephant (n)
njogu ni inene an elephant is very big

njointi joint (n)
kuucia jointi ciaku stretch your joints

njoka snake (n)
njoka iti maguru a snake has no legs

Njuma Saturday (n)
day of the week *Ciana cia Njuma* Saturday children

njuno fable (n)
atiitikagia njuno one does not believe fables

nkaatho praise (n)
niabaterie nkaatho she deserves praise

nkai groin (n)
nkai cia muntu-murume groin of a man

nkai penis (n)
u tiumba kuuga "nkai" mbere ya kirindi you don't say 'penis' in public

nkamira camel (n)
nkamira ithanthatu six camels

nkara egg (n)
nkara ya nguku chicken egg

nkathi ladder (n)
nkathi indaaja long ladder

nkiaa indigent (n)
nkiaa iti gantu an indigent has nothing

nkingo neck (n)
Tai ikaraga nkingo the tie hangs on his neck

nkingo neck (n)
tai icuraga nkingo the tie hangs on his neck

nkobia hat (n)
Ni ekirite nkobia he is wearing a hat

nkoro soul (n)
nkoro yakwa ni iguukiiria my soul exults

nkoro heart (n)
nkoro injega good heart

nkuaa armpit (n)
nkuaa ikununka smelly armpit

nkunia sack (n)
guti gintu kiri ndene ya nkunia yakwa nothing inside my sack

nkunkwa orange (n)
makunkwa jathatu three oranges

nkuru tortoise (n)
nkuru itaga kaora a tortoise walks slowly

nkuruki than (conj)
ni umuraja nkuruki yakwa he is taller than me

nkuu firewood (n)
jukia nkuu pickup firewood

ntaka mud (n)
Thambia ntaka wash the mud

ntanta drop (n)
nguku inyunyaga ruuji ntanta na ntanta drop by drop a chicken drinks water

ntariki date (v)
ugampa ntariki will you date me?

ntariki date (n)
Narua i ntariki ingana? which date is today?

nteremente toffee (n)
ria nteremente lick a toffee

nthao disgrace (n)
aibu na nthao shame and disgrace

nthata barren (adj)
muntu-muka nthata barren woman

nthiguru nation (n)
nthiguru yako your nation

nthiguru world (n)
twana twa nthiguru children of the world

nthiguru country (n)
nthiguru yaku your country

nthiguru floor (n)
nthiguru on the floor

nthii down (adv)
ita nthii go down

nthii earth (n)
antu ba nthii people of the earth

nthingiri ant (n)
nthingiri ngiri thousands of ants

nthongi nice (adj)
mithithie itwike inthongi make it nice

nthoroko bean (n)
mucere na nthoroko rice and beans

nthua louse (n)
nthua cia nguku chicken lice

ntigwa widowed (adj)
ntumurume ntigwa widowed man

ntina not have (v)
ntina mbeca indi ndina utonga I don't have money but I have property

ntiri mortar (n)
muti na ntiri pestle and mortar

ntuku day (n)
ntuku igukinya the day has arrived

ntuku cionthe daily (adv)
ejaga aja ntuku cionthe he comes here daily

ntuku inyanya eight days (n)
eteera ntuku inyanya wait eight days

ntuku ya guciarwa birthday (n)
Narua ni ntuku ya guciarwa yakwa today is my birthday

ntumurume man (n)
ntumurume u muraaja a tall man

ntumurume male (n)
Mandela ni ntumurume Mandela is male

ntumurume man (n)
ntumurume u muraja a tall man

ntumwa message (n)
riria ntumwa yakinyire when the message arrived

ntunda fruit (n)
tua ntunda pluck fruit

ntuntuguru owl (n)
ntuntuguru ni nyoni an owl is a bird

ntura neighbourhood (n)
ntukaraga ntura imwe we live in the same neighbourhood

ntuti suddenly (adv)
yejire ntuti it came suddenly

ntuti quickly (adv)
ita ntuti you walk quickly

ntuti immediately (adv)
tigana nayo ntuti cut off immediately

nusu ya kilo gram (n)
nusu ikumi cia kilo ten grams

nyaki grass (n)
ng'ombe ithagumagia nyaki a

cow chews grass
nyaki grass (n)
 ngombe irijaga nyaki a cow chews grass
nyama beef (n)
 ria nyama eat beef
nyama meat (n)
 nyama ya mburi goat meat
nyama ya ngurwe pork (n)
 nyama ya ngurwe iri na murio pork is tasty
nyanya tomato (n)
 nyanya ijiri two tomatoes
nyingi many (adj)
 ngari i nyingi many vehicles
nyiuru nose (n)
 gutu na nyiuru ear and nose
nyomba house (n)
 nyomba the house
nyomba ya kuthambira bathroom (n)
 Ita nyomba ya kuthambira go to the bathroom
nyomba ya mbunge parliament house (n)
 kumuthura gwita nyomba ya mbunge elect her to go to parliament house
nyomba ya ngoroba storey building (n)
 ningwaka nyomba ya ngoroba I am building a storey building
nyongu pot (n)
 nyongu ya cuuma metal pot
nyoni bird (n)
 nyoni ikuburuka a bird flies

nyonta thirst (n)
 ndina nyonta I feel thirst (I am thirsty)
nyonto breast (n)
 iria ria nyonto breast milk
nyoroco leopard (n)
 nyoroco iri na muthirinya a leopard has a tail
nyuma behind (prep)
 ita nyuma go behind
nyuma ya nyomba backyard (n)
 nyuma ya nyomba ikugia iria mono the backyard is overgrown

O, o

omba maybe (adv)
 omba kwija maybe he will come
oria extinguish (v)
 oria rumuri extinguish the flame
oria heal (v)
 kuoria murimo heal disease
ou as (adv)
 ou i kari as it is

P, p

pinki pink (adj)
 ngurwe imwe ni cia rangi ya pinki some pigs are pink
pointi full stop (n)
 imwe pointi ithano ni nusu 1.5 is one and a half.
printa printer (n)
 printa ya mauku book printer

printi print (v)
  printi barua print the email

R, r

raisi easy (adj)
  kigeranio kiri raisi the exam is easy
raisi cheap (adj)
  kuithirwa raisi be cheap
rangi ink (n)
  rangi ya karamu ink in a pen
rangi ya mathangu greenish (adj)
  nyomba iri na rangi ya mathangu greenish house
rangira guard (v)
  rangira nyomba guard the house
ria pay (v)
  nkaria I will pay
ria eat (v)
  ku ria bionthe to eat everything
riboti report (n)
  thithia riboti make a report
riganirua forget (v)
  nkuriganirua I have forgotten
riikone kitchen (n)
  ndi riikone I am in the kitchen
riitho eye (n)
  riitho eye and eyebrow
riitho eyeball (n)
  riitho eye and eyeball
riitwa name (n)
  riitwa riaku my name
riko kitchen (n)
  ndi rikone I am in the kitchen

ringa click (v)
  ringa aja click here
ringa mbica draw (v)
  ringa mbica ya nyoni draw a bird

ringa mpii clap (v)
  kuringa mpii cia Yaa to clap for Yaa
rĩngĩ again (adv)
  muone rĩngĩ see her again
rira cry (v)
  rira igita rionthe to cry each time

ritithia email (n)
  ritithia baruga e rugo print the email
riu then (adv)
  riu aramama then he slept
riua sun (n)
  riua ni rikwara the sun is shining

romba pray (v)
  romba niuntu bwa antu bakwa to pray for my enemies
romba beg (v)
  kuromba gintu beg for something

romba borrow (v)
  romba mbeca borrow money
rota dream (v)
  kurota mono to dream a lot
rubau plank (n)
  rubau na musumari plank and nail
rubunguro key (n)
  murango na rubunguro door and

key

ruga cook (v)
ruga mucere jumukai cook a little rice

ruga make (v)
ruga irio make food

ruga bake (v)
ruga mugate bake bread

rugai inheritance (n)
tetera rugai rwaku claim your inheritance

rugono blog (n)
rugono rwa irio food blog

rugono rwa karaja history (n)
thoma rugono rwa karaja learn history

rugura open (v)
nkurugura mwari I open the door

ruguru north (adj)
ita bwa ruguru go north

Rui blow (n)
muringe rui give him a blow

ruko dishevelled (adj)
muntu o ruko dishevelled self

ruma insult (v)
tiga kumuruma stop insulting her

ruma bite (v)
kuru yomba ku ruma the dog can bite

ruma insult (n)
irumi bibiingi many insults

rumena hatred (n)
rumena ruti mutheega hatred has no cure

rungika brake (v)
ndereva akurungika ngari the driver has braked

rūraya abroad (n)
Nĩathiaga rūraya she goes abroad

rurigi string (n)
rurigi na sindano string and needle

ruuji water (n)
nyua ruuji you drink water

ruuju tomorrow (adv)
agakinya ruuju she will arrive tomorrow

ruukiri morning (n)
ruukiri kiroko early morning

ruukiri early (adj)
ruukiri kiroko early morning

ruukiri kiroko dawn (n)
ruukiri kiroko thaa kumi na ijiri 6am

ruuko filthy (adj)
kuri na ruuko the place is filthy

ruumu ya kumama bedroom (n)
nyomba iri na ruumu cia kumama ijiri the house has two bedrooms

ruuo wind (n)
ruuo ni rikuurutana the wind is blowing

rwagi mosquito (n)
rwagi rukunduma a mosquito has bitten me

rwanda desert (n)
rwanda guti ruuji water is scarce

in the desert
rwego fence (n)
nyuma ya rwego behind a fence
rwembeeria gutter (n)
kurina ruuji kiri rwembeeria there is water in the gutter
rwemberiene ledge (n)
mama rwemberiene sleep on the ledge
rwiro race (n)
ugia rwiro run a race
rwongo abroad (n)
Nietaga rwongo she goes abroad

S, s

senema cinema (n)
mbitite senema I am going to a cinema
siasa politics (n)
wendete siasa you like politics
simiti cement (n)
maiga na simiti stones and cement

sindano needle (n)
rurigi na sindano string and needle
sinema cinema (n)
Mbitite kwona sinema I am going to a cinema
siri password (n)
Garura siri change password
starehe luxury (n)
Ndiona starehe maishene jaku ja nau mbere I see luxury in your future

T, t

ta discard (v)
ta mubira discard the ball
taika vomit (n)
mataika ja kuru dog's vomit
takuna chew (v)
gutakuna nchugu to chew groundnuts
tambarare flat (adj)
metha tambarare flat table
tandika lantern (n)
gwatia tandika turn on the lantern
tanga harass (v)
ni uguntanga you are harassing me
tanga hassle (v)
kumutanga kenda aria hassle him so that he pays
tara count (v)
tara mbeca count money
tayari ready (adv)
ndi tayari I am ready
tega kuraja look away (v)
ningutega kuraja I look away
teta quarrel (n)
iteta ririnene a big quarrel
thaa ii now (adv)
ita thaa ii go now
thaa ingi later (adv)
bakaria thaa ingi they will eat later
thaa inyanya afternoon (n)
nkeeja thaa inyanya I will come in the afternoon

thaabu   gold (n)
miruki i mithongi na thaabu fragrance and gold

thaaka   cast (n)
thaaka itinda cast of a film

thaani   plate (n)
thambia thaani yaku wash your plate

thamba   bath (v)
kuthamba o rukiri runthe to bath each morning

thambia   clean (v)
thambia maigo jaku clean your teeth

thara   grab (v)
thara njara yawe grab his hand

tharike   blood (n)
ruuji na tharike water and blood

tharima   bless (v)
ntharima bless me

theruka   boil (v)
subu ni ikutheruka the soup is boiling

thia   grind (v)
kuthia mpempe to grind corn

thigara   cigarette (n)
nyua thigara smoke a cigarette

thigiriri   ant (n)
Makiri ma thigiriri thousands of ants

thiina   plague (n)
guti thiina aja no plagues there

thiiri   peace (n)
ndienda thiiri I want peace

thika   bury (v)
thika kiimba bury a corpse

thikiria   listen (v)
kuthikiria rwimbo to listen to music

thingata   follow (v)
nthingata follow me

thinka   doze (v)
niukuthinka you are dozing

thiria   pacify (v)
thiria ndua pacify the fight

thoko   market (n)
ita thoko go to market

thoma   learn (v)
thoma mugambo they learn a language

thugania   figure (v)
uri thugania ni bu buumo you figure it is hard?

thukia   defile (v)
ugacithukia do not defile yourself

thungutha   jump (v)
kuthungutha ruthingo to jump a wall

thura   hate (v)
kuthura uthao to hate laziness

thuura   nominate (v)
thuura igita name a time

thuuta   climb (v)
thuuta irima to climb mountains

tia   honour (v)
tia Ngai honour the Lord

tigiti   ticket (n)
tega tigiti yakwa look at my ticket

tinga   except (conj)
tinga Ngai except God

tiria cancel (v)
  tiria mucemanio cancel the meeting

tirima bump into (v)
  ngari igutirima gintu the car has bumped into something

tirima meet (v)
  ntirima nja meet me at home

toi smoke (n)
  kurita toi belch smoke

tonya enter (v)
  tonya nyomba enter into the room

tumiiria announce (v)
  tumiiria atiri announce that

tura pierce (v)
  tura matu jaku pierce your ear

U, u

uciathi independence (n)
  ntuku ya uciathi independence day

ucuru porridge (n)
  ucuru bwa ugimbi millet porridge

ugia mai fart (v)
  muntu akugia mai someone has farted

ugima bwa mwiri health (n)
  irio biejaga muntu ugima mwa mwiri food gives health

ugimbi millet (n)
  ucuru bwa ugimbi millet porridge

ugoro evening (n)
  irio bia ugoro; irio evening meal; dinner

uguri price (n)
  uguri bwayo its price?

uguriruo revelation (n)
  niari na uguriruo he had a revelation

ugwaa fear (n)
  ugwaa buujirite nkoro yawe fear has filled her heart

ugwati chaotic (adj)
  guntu kuri na ugwati the place is chaotic

uhuru liberty (n)
  turi na uhuru we have liberty

Ũ, ũ

Ũithĩramu Islam (n)
  Ũkristo na Ũithĩramu Christianity and Islam

U, u

ujuria fill (v)
  ujuria iu fill it

ujuria fill up (v)
  ujuria itangi fill up the barrel

uki honey (n)
  uki buri na murio honey is sweet

ukia covetuousness (n)
  ukia butibui covetuousness is not good

ukia poverty (n)
ukia kana utonga poverty or wealth

ukiiria exult (v)
nkoro yakwa igukiiria my soul exults

ukiria lift (v)
ukiria iguru to lift higher

uma tharike bleed (v)
ni akuma tharike he is bleeding

umiiria encourage (v)
mue kuumiiria encourage her

umithio consequence (n)
umithio bwayo its consequences

umuntu human ()
turi na umuntu we are humans

umutho left (adj)
ita ruteere rwa umutho go left

umuthongi pretty (adj)
muntu muka umuthongi a pretty woman

umwe one (p)
umwe atitikanitie na ngono iu one does not believe fables

una break (v)
una muti break the stick

ungania mix (v)
ungania nyanya na ncini to mix tomatoes and pepper

unthu enmity (n)
unthu bubunene great enmity

untu issue (n)
untu bubueru new issue

untu issue (n)
untu buu bweru new issue

ura get lost (v)
ura uri tauni to get lost in town

uraga murder (n)
kuguuta na kuraga gossip and murder

uraga kill (v)
uraga mburi to kill a goat

urekaniri forgiveness (n)
wendo, witikio na urekaniri love, acceptance and forgiveness

uri na inya powerful (adj)
kiroria uri na inya powerful prophet

uria ask (v)
uria Kofi ask Kofi

urio east (adj)
ita urio go east

urio right (adj)
ita urio go right

urongo lie (n)
urongo na ukora lies and discord

urongo deception (n)
urongo na kurega kugwatanira deception and discord

ururu painful (adj)
mbajua iri ururu illness is painful

urururu pain (n)
urururu buri aja the pain is here

utethio help (n)
muntu wonthe niendete utethio everyone needs help

utheri mere (adj)
kiaa utheri mere fool

uthiu forehead (n)
tega uthiu bwawe look at her fore-

head

uthiu face (n)
tega uthiu bwakwa *look at my face*

uthongi fetish (n)
tauni iiji iri na uthongi *this town has a fetish*

uthongi beauty (n)
Uthongi na wendo *beauty and love*

uthuku evil (n)
ni uthuku buriku buubu? *which evil is this?*

uthurania gather (v)
uthurania antu bonthe *gather everyone*

uthurania collect (v)
kuthurania mbeca *to collect money*

utuku nightfall (n)
muthenya na utuku *daybreak and nightfall*

utuku night (n)
thaa ijiri cia utuku *8 o'clock in the night*

utuuro life (n)
tura utuuro bwaku *live your life well*

uu that (conj)
nidikuga uu *I say that*

uu who (p)
nuu uu? *who is he?*

uugira blow (v)
uugira miruki *blow air*

uuma rangi fade (v)
ngui ikuuma rangi *the cloth has*

faded

uumba create (v)
uumba gintu gikieru *create something new*

uume knowledge (n)
uume bunthe thigurune *all knowledge in the world*

uuna cross (v)
uuna ruuji *cross the stream*

W, w

waa folly (n)
ni waa butheri *it is just folly*

Waĩrĩ Tuesday (n)
ciana cia Waĩrĩ *Tuesday children*

wamba burglary (n)
wamba bukuingia *burglary is increasing*

watho law (n)
watho bugite *the law says*

we her (p)
nyomba yawe *her house*

we his (p)
nyomba ya we *his house*

we he (p)
we niarijaga *he eats*

wembe razor (n)
noora wembe *sharpen the razor*

Wena Thursday (n)
ciana cia Wena *Thursday children*

wendi will (n)
wendi bwa Ngai *God's will*

wendo love (n)
  wendo na thiiri love and peace
wengwa yourselves (p)
  cimenyere wengwa bwega look
  after yourselves well
wengwa herself (p)
  niaciete gitio wengwa shc respects herself
wengwa himself (p)
  niaciete gitio wengwa he respects
  himself
wenka only (adj)
  ugwe wenka only you
weru light (n)
  weru bwa iguru light of the sky
Wetano Friday (n)
  Ciana cia Wetano Friday children

Wetatũ Wednesday (n)
  ciana cia Wetatũ Wednesday children
wingi plenty (adj)
  mauntu ja maingi plenty of issues

wirane promise (n)
  mpa wirane give me a promise
wirane promise (v)
  mpa wirane promise me
wirane testament (n)
  wirane bu bweru new testament
wirigiro hope (n)
  ndina wirigiro I have hope
witikio faith (n)
  witikio na thiiri faith and peace

yakwa mine (p)
  ni biakwa this thing is mine
yawe hers (p)
  iji ni yawe this thing is hers
yetu our (p)
  nyomba yetu our house
yetu ours (p)
  uuni na Kofi, iji ni yetu I and Kofi,
  this thing is ours
yiumba creation (n)
  yiumba rionthe all creation
yonthe entire (adj)
  nyomba yonthe the entire house
yonthe totally (adv)
  yonthe ni iire it is totally burnt

Y, y

ENGLISH-GIKUYU
Index

a, xv
abdomen *kiu*, 13
abdomen *nda*, 26
abroad *rwongo*, 34
abroad *rūraya*, 33
accept *itikiira*, 10
addition *gūtaranīria*, 6
adjectives, xiii, xxi
adult *muntu mugima*, 22
adult *mūgima*, 20
Adverbs, xxi
adverbs, xxi
advice *mataaro*, 18
advice *mataro*, 18
aeroplane *ndege*, 26
Africa *Afrika*, 1
African *Mwafrica*, 24
African *Mūafrika*, 20
afternoon *thaa inyanya*, 34
again *kairi*, 10
again *rīngī*, 32
alert *menyithia*, 19
all *bionthe*, 2
all *ciothe*, 3

alligator *mamba*, 17
alligator *nchana*, 26
allow *itikiira*, 9
almighty *kīhoti-othe*, 12
almighty *munene*, 21
alphabet, ix
amazing *kurigarania*, 15
amazing *kūgegania*, 14
amongst *gatagatī-inī ka*, 4
amongst *gatigati*, 4
amusing *gūkenania*, 5
amusing *kugegania*, 14
an, xv
ancestor *bajuuju batene*, 2
ancestor *maguka ma tene*, 17
and *na*, 26
anger *marakara*, 18
announce *tumiiria*, 36
announcement *manīrīra*, 17
annoying *kuthuria*, 16
annoying *kūrakaria*, 15
annul *kuthiria*, 16
answer *icokio*, 7
ant *nthingiri*, 30

ant *thigiriri*, 35
apparition *irundu bia akuu*, 9
appreciate *kugwirirua*, 14
April *Mweri jwa Ina*, 25
April *Mũthaatũ*, 23
argue *guteta*, 6
argument *macokanĩrio*, 17
argument *mateta*, 18
arm *njara*, 28
armpit *nkuaa*, 29
arrange *banga*, 2
arrive *kinya*, 12
as *ou*, 31
ash *muthetu*, 23
ask *uria*, 37
association *ngwataniro*, 28
attach *gwatithania*, 6
attire *nguo*, 28
August *Mweri jwa inana*, 25
August *Mũgiranjara*, 20
award *kiewa*, 12

baby *mwana*, 24
backyard *nyuma ya nyomba*, 31
bad *inthuku*, 8
bag *kiondo*, 12
bake *ruga*, 33
ball *mubira*, 20
balloon *mbaluni*, 18
banana *irigu*, 8
baptise *batithia*, 2
bargain *ariiria*, 1
bark *gamba*, 4
barrel *mutungi*, 24
barren *nthata*, 29
basket *kitheti*, 13
bath *thamba*, 35

bathroom *nyomba ya kuthambira*, 31
battle *kurua*, 15
battle *ndua*, 27
battle *ndwaa*, 27
be able to *ndomba*, 27
be guilty of *kuigua bui*, 14
be ill *kuigua bubui*, 14
be jealous *igua ruriitho*, 7
be pregnant *gia iu*, 4
be shy *kuigua nthoni*, 14
be wrong *itia*, 9
bean *nthoroko*, 30
bear fruit *kugia matunda*, 14
beard *kireru*, 13
beat *kuura*, 16
beautiful *i nthongi*, 7
beauty *uthongi*, 38
because *niuntu*, 28
become famous *kumenyeka*, 14
bed *gitanda*, 5
bedroom *ruumu ya kumama*, 33
beef *nyama*, 31
befit *nganira*, 27
before *mbere*, 18
befriend *guciendithia*, 5
beg *romba*, 32
begin *ambiiria*, 1
behind *nyuma*, 31
being *kwithirwa*, 16
belch *enketha*, 3
believe *itikia*, 9
beloved *mwendwa wakwa*, 25
bend *kunja*, 15
betray *kunyanira*, 15
bicycle *baisikili*, 2

big *nene*, 27
bird *nyoni*, 31
birthday *ntuku ya guciarwa*, 30
bishop *mutumiria*, 23
bite *ruma*, 33
bitter *ng´ana*, 27
black *i njiru*, 7
blanket *muringiti*, 22
blazing *gwakana*, 6
bleed *uma tharike*, 37
bleeding *kuuma tharike*, 16
bless *tharima*, 35
blessing *itharimo*, 9
blog *rugono*, 33
blood *tharike*, 35
blow *Rui*, 33
blow *uugira*, 38
blowfly *ngii*, 27
blue *mbluu*, 18
boat *gitaru*, 5
bodice *kauna*, 11
boil *iuti*, 10
boil *theruka*, 35
book *ibuku*, 7
book *iuku*, 10
borrow *romba*, 32
bother *guntanga*, 6
bother *gusumbura*, 6
bother *gutanga*, 6
bottle *cuuba*, 3
bow-legged *ngecere*, 27
box *mbogisi*, 19
boy *kaiji*, 10
brake *rungika*, 33
branch *athukira*, 1
bread *mugate*, 20

break *una*, 37
breast *nyonto*, 31
breath *miruki*, 19
breathe *ikia miruki*, 7
bride *muiki*, 21
bright *iri na utheri*, 8
broom *kiegeri*, 12
broomstick *muti jwa kiegeri*, 23
brother *mutanocia*, 23
brown *muthetu*, 23
bruise *ngara*, 27
bucket *mutungi*, 24
bud *mucoriru*, 20
build *aka*, 1
bump into *tirima*, 36
burglary *wamba*, 38
burn *ithia*, 9
bury *thika*, 35
bush *mwitu*, 26
but *indi*, 8
butterfly *kiragutia*, 13
buttocks *maindi*, 17
buy *gura*, 6
by any chance *kwombika*, 16

calf *kajau*, 10
call *ita*, 9
camel *nkamira*, 29
camera *kamera*, 11
cancel *tiria*, 36
car *ngari*, 27
caress *kugwatagwata*, 14
carve *kuma*, 14
cassava *mukwacii*, 21
cast *athaki*, 1
cast *thaaka*, 35
castanet *kayamba*, 11

43

cat *mpaka*, 19
catch *gwata*, 6
cement *cimiti*, 3
cement *simiti*, 34
chair *giti*, 5
change *chenji*, 3
change *garuka*, 4
chaotic *ugwati*, 36
character *mitugo*, 19
charcoal *makara*, 17
chase *inga*, 8
cheap *raisi*, 32
chest *kibara*, 12
chew *takuna*, 34
chieftain *murugi*, 22
child *mwana*, 24
Christian *mukiristu*, 21
church *kanisa*, 11
cigarette *thigara*, 35
cinema *senema*, 34
cinema *sinema*, 34
citizen *mwananchi*, 24
clap *ringa mpii*, 32
clay *muthetu jwa yumba*, 23
clean *thambia*, 35
clear *egera*, 3
clearly *bubuega*, 2
clearly *bwega*, 2
click *ringa*, 32
climb *thuuta*, 35
close *inga*, 8
cloth *gitambaa*, 5
clothes *nguo*, 28
cloud *ituu*, 10
coach *kochi*, 13
cocoa *kokoa*, 13

cocoyam leaves *mathangu ja kokoyamu*, 18
coin *kingotore*, 12
cold *mpio*, 20
cold temperature *mpio*, 20
collander *mpakuri*, 19
collect *uthurania*, 38
comb *canura*, 2
comb *gichanuri*, 4
come *ija*, 7
comfort *kuumiriria*, 16
commend *kaatha*, 10
compensation *marii*, 18
competition *macindano*, 17
competition *mashindano*, 18
concord, x
concubine *munyanya*, 22
Conjunctions, xxiii
consequence *umithio*, 37
continue *itanambere*, 9
cook *ruga*, 33
cool *igwe mpio*, 7
coop *kiugu*, 13
corn *mpempe*, 19
corners *kona*, 13
corpse *kiimba*, 12
cough *korora*, 13
count *tara*, 34
country *nthiguru*, 30
court *igoti*, 7
court *koti*, 13
cover *kunika*, 15
covetuousness *ukia*, 36
cow *ngombe*, 28
cowhide *muguuta jwa ngombe*, 20
crab *kingangiri*, 12

44

each and everyone *bonthe*, 2
ear *gutu*, 6
early *kurio*, 15
early *ruukiri*, 33
earpiece *gatu ga gwikira matu*, 4
earth *nthii*, 30
earthquake *kwinaina kwa nthig-uru*, 16
east *urio*, 37
easy *raisi*, 32
eat *ria*, 32
education *kithomo*, 13
effort *inya*, 8
egg *nkara*, 29
eight *inyanya*, 8
eight days *ntuku inyanya*, 30
eight persons *antu banaana*, 1
eighteen *ikumi na inyanya*, 7
elastic *muubira*, 24
elder *mukuru*, 21
elephant *njogu*, 28
eleven *ikumi na imwe*, 7
email *ritithia*, 32
embrace *cuncha*, 3
empathy *kiao*, 11
encourage *umiiria*, 37
encouragement *kuumiriria*, 16
end *muthia*, 23
enemy *munthu*, 21
English *Gicunku*, 4
English *Gĩthũngũ*, 5
enmity *unthu*, 37
enter *tonya*, 36
entertaining *gukenia*, 5
entire *yonthe*, 39
equal *kung`anana*, 15

evening *ugoro*, 36
event *kiatho*, 12
everyone *bonthe*, 2
everything *bionthe*, 2
everywhere *kunthe*, 15
evil *uthuku*, 38
exam *kigeranio*, 12
except *tinga*, 35
explain *ereithia*, 3
extinguish *oria*, 31
exult *ukiiria*, 37
exultation *gukaatha*, 5
eye *riitho*, 32
eyeball *riitho*, 32
eyebrow *nciuri cia riitho*, 26

fable *njuno*, 28
fabric *gitambaa*, 5
face *uthiu*, 38
fade *uuma rangi*, 38
faith *witikio*, 39
fall down *guaa nthi*, 5
fall into *guaa ndene*, 5
falsification *kuandanira*, 13
family *famili*, 3
farm *muunda*, 24
farmer *mkulima*, 19
fart *kuugia mai*, 16
fart *ugia mai*, 36
fast *guciata*, 5
father *ithe*, 9
favoritism *kimenyano*, 12
fear *gukira*, 5
fear *ugwaa*, 36
feather *mbui*, 19
February *Mweri jwa iri*, 25
February *Mũgetho*, 20

give birth *gia*, 4
go *ita*, 9
go to the toilet *ita kioro*, 9
goat *mburi*, 19
god *mirugu*, 19
gold *thaabu*, 35
gong gong *ngong ngong*, 28
good *gikiega*, 4
good friend *mucore umwega*, 20
goosebumps *kigimbi*, 12
gossip *guta*, 6
gossip *ngutu*, 28
govern *atha*, 1
grab *thara*, 35
gram *nusu ya kilo*, 30
grammar, ix
grass *nyaki*, 30, 31
grease *maguta ja ngirisi*, 17
great *nene*, 27
greenish *rangi ya mathangu*, 32
greet *kethia*, 11
grief *kuithikira*, 14
grieve *ithikira*, 9
grind *thia*, 35
groin *nkai*, 29
groom *mugurani*, 20
groom *muikithania*, 21
groundnut *ncugu*, 26
group *gikundi*, 4
grove *gikundi*, 4
grow *gukura*, 6
guard *rangira*, 32
guest *mugeni*, 20
gutter *rwembeeria*, 34

habitual tense, xviii
habit *mitugo*, 19

habitat *gikaro*, 4
hair *nchiuri*, 26
hand *njara*, 28
hang *cuuria*, 3
happiness *gikeno*, 4
harass *tanga*, 34
hassle *tanga*, 34
hat *nkobia*, 29
hate *thura*, 35
hatred *rumena* , 33
have a hold on *kungwata*, 15
hawk *kwendia*, 16
he *we*, 38
head *kiongo*, 12
headache *mutwe*, 24
headgear *gitambaa gia kiongo*, 5
heading *kiongone*, 12
heal *oria*, 31
health *ugima bwa mwiri*, 36
heart *nkoro*, 29
heavy *ndito*, 27
heel *gikinya*, 4
help *utethio*, 37
her *we*, 38
hers *yawe*, 39
herself *wengwa*, 39
hiccups *gwenketha*, 6
hill *kirima*, 13
himself *wengwa*, 39
his *we*, 38
history *rugono rwa karaja*, 33
hoe *irinya*, 9
hold *gwata*, 6
hole *irinya*, 9
holy *kuthera*, 15
home *njaa*, 28

honey *uki*, 36
honour *tia*, 35
hope *wirigiro*, 39
horse *mbarathi*, 18
hospital *cibitari*, 3
hot *mwanki*, 25
hotel *mukawa*, 21
hour *ithaa*, 9
house *nyomba*, 31
housefly *ngii*, 28
how *atia*, 1
how much *ing`ana*, 8
human *umuntu*, 37
humankind *antu*, 1
humility *kwinyiha*, 16
hunger *mpara*, 19
husband *mukuru*, 21

I *nii*, 28
if *kethira*, 11
immediately *ntuti*, 30
imperative sentences, xxi
in *ndene*, 27
in front *mbere*, 18
in that case *niuntu buu*, 28
in-law *antu betu*, 1
inactive *kithao*, 13
increase *ingia*, 8
indefinite articles, xv
independence *uciathi*, 36
indigent *nkiaa*, 29
indigo *indigo*, 8
inheritance *rugai*, 33
inject *munta*, 21
injection *kumuntwa cindano*, 15
ink *rangi*, 32
inside *ndene*, 27

insult *ruma*, 33
interrogative sentences, xxi
Islam *Isilamu*, 9
Islam *Ũithĩramu*, 36
island *irigiritwe na iria*, 8
issue *untu*, 37
it *iu*, 10
ivory *mugwongo*, 21

jail *nceera*, 26
jama *jama*, 10
January *Mweri jwa mwambirio*, 25
January *Mũgaa*, 20
jar *mutungi*, 24
joint *njointi*, 28
jollof *jollof*, 10
journalist *muaandiki*, 20
judge *mugambi*, 20
judgement *kugitirwa igamba*, 14
July *Muoria Nyoni*, 22
July *Mweri jwa mugwanja*, 25
jump *thungutha*, 35
June *Gacicia*, 3
June *Mweri jwa itantatu*, 25
junk *mati*, 18
just *aki*, 1
just *au*, 1

ka, xx
karĩa, xv
kau, xv
key *rubunguro*, 32
keyboard *kibodi*, 12
khebab *kebab*, 11
kill *uraga*, 37
kilometer *kilomita*, 12
kilometre *kilomita*, 12

kindle *gwatia*, 6
king *munene*, 21
kiss *cunca*, 3
kitchen *riikone*, 32
kitchen *riko*, 32
knee *iru*, 9
knife *gaciu*, 4
know *menya*, 19
knowledge *uume*, 38

ladder *nkathi*, 29
lake *leki*, 17
land *munda*, 21
language *mugambo*, 20
lantern *tandika*, 34
later *thaa ingi*, 34
lavatory *bathurumu*, 2
law *watho*, 38
lazy *muthao*, 23
leader *mutongeria*, 23
leaf *ithangu*, 9
leak *gwitura*, 6
lean on *mamira*, 17
learn *thoma*, 35
ledge *rwemberiene*, 34
left *umutho*, 37
leg *kuguru*, 14
lend *a*, 1
leniency *kiao*, 11
lens *meetho*, 19
leopard *nyoroco*, 31
let *ga*, 3
liar *murongo*, 22
liberty *uhuru*, 36
lick *cuna*, 3
lie *urongo*, 37
life *utuuro*, 38

lift *ukiria*, 37
light *weru*, 39
lime *ndimu*, 27
lion *ngatunyi*, 27
lips *miromo*, 19
liquor *ncoobi*, 26
listen *thikiria*, 35
listener *muthikiri*, 23
little *niini*, 28
living *mwoyo*, 26
living room *meethene*, 19
lizard *murururu*, 23
loan *kobithia*, 13
loan *mukobo*, 21
logo *logo*, 17
long *indaaja*, 8
look away *tega kuraja*, 34
look for *cwaa*, 3
lorry *lori*, 17
louse *nthua*, 30
love *enda*, 3
love *wendo*, 39
luxury *mwago*, 24
luxury *starehe*, 34

machine *mashini*, 18
madam *mandamu*, 17
maid *muriti wa ngugi*, 22
make *ruga*, 33
male *ntumurume*, 30
man *ntumurume*, 30
mango *iembe*, 7
manner *mitugo*, 19
many *nyingi*, 31
march *cenca*, 2
March *Kĩhu*, 12
market *thoko*, 35

marriage *kugurana*, 14
marry *gura*, 6
master *muntu*, 22
mat *mugeka*, 20
May *Gĩthathanwa*, 5
maybe *omba*, 31
meat *nyama*, 31
medicine *daawa*, 3
medicine *ndawa*, 26
meet *tirima*, 36
meeting *mucemanio*, 20
melt *eruka*, 3
memorization *kumemorise*, 14
memorize *ikira kiongo*, 7
mere *utheri*, 37
message *ntumwa*, 30
messenger *mutumwa*, 24
metal *cuuma*, 3
metal *ncuma*, 26
meter *mita*, 19
metre *mita*, 19
middle *gatigati*, 4
mile *maili*, 17
millet *ugimbi*, 36
mind *kiongo*, 12
mine *yakwa*, 39
minute *ndagika*, 26
mirror *kioni*, 13
miserly *ngoga*, 28
miss *mwari*, 25
missus *mwekuru*, 25
mist *nduume*, 27
mistake *makosa*, 17
mix *ungania*, 37
Modern Gikuyu, vii
moment *igiita*, 7

Monday *Jumatatũ*, 10
Monday *Muthenya jwa mwambirio jwa kiumia*, 23
money *mbeca*, 18
monkey *iruki*, 9
month *mweri*, 25
moon *mweri*, 25
morning *ruukiri*, 33
mortar *ntiri*, 30
mosquito *rwagi*, 33
mother *mami*, 17
mountain *kirima*, 13
mouse *mbea*, 18
mouth *muromo*, 22
mud *ntaka*, 29
multiplication *kuugithia mainda*, 16
murder *uraga*, 37
murderer *muragani*, 22
murderer *muuragani*, 24
mushroom *makunu*, 17
music *musiki*, 23
musician *mũini*, 21
myself *ningwa*, 28

nail *mucumari*, 20
name *riitwa*, 32
nation *nthiguru*, 29
neck *nkingo*, 29
necklace *mukathi*, 21
need *kwenda*, 16
needle *sindano*, 34
neighbourhood *ntura*, 30
new *injeru*, 8
news *imenyithia*, 7
nice *nthongi*, 30
niece *kaari ka mwariocia*, 10

54

http://kasahorow.org/gikuyu

0-7 years

> My First Gikuyu Counting Book
> My First Gikuyu Dictionary

8-12 years

> 102 Gikuyu Verbs
> Gikuyu Children's Dictionary

12+ years

> Modern Gikuyu
> Gikuyu Learner's Dictionary
> Modern Gikuyu Dictionary
> Waikeno.com

Made in the USA
Middletown, DE
23 November 2015